WINDOWS TO
ETERNITY

WINDOWS TO ETERNITY

JENNY
ROBERTSON

Published by
The Bible Reading Fellowship
Peter's Way, Sandy Lane West
Oxford OX4 5HG
ISBN 1 84101 045 6

First published 1999
10 9 8 7 6 5 4 3 2 1 0

Acknowledgments
Unless otherwise stated, biblical quotations are taken from the New Revised
Standard Version of the Bible, copyright © 1989, 1995 by the Division of
Christian Education of the National Council of the Churches of Christ in the
United States of America, and are used by permission. All rights reserved.

Scripture quotations taken from the Holy Bible, New International Version, copyright © 1973, 1978, 1984 by International Bible Society, are used by permission
of Hodder & Stoughton Ltd. All rights reserved. 'NIV' is a registered trademark
of International Bible Society. UK trademark 1448790.

Scriptures quoted from the Good News Bible published by the Bible Societies/
HarperCollins Publishers Ltd, UK © American Bible Society 1966, 1971, 1976,
1992, used with permission.

Scriptures quoted from the New King James Version of the Bible © 1979, 1980,
1982 by Thomas Nelson, Inc. Used by permission. All rights reserved.

'Rublev's Icon' quoted by permission of John Bate. Extract from *The Coming of
God* by Maria Boulding used by permission of Dame Maria Boulding and SPCK.
Extract from *The Way of a Pilgrim*, trs. R.M. French (SPCK), used by permission.
Passages quoted from *Religion in Communist Lands*, the journal of Keston College,
the research and information centre on religion in communist and post-
communist countries. Since 1992 the Keston journal has continued publication
as *Religion, State and Society*, and Keston College continues its work as Keston
Institute in Oxford. Extracts from *Christianity for the Twenty-First Century: The Life
and Work of Alexander Men*, ed. Elizabeth Roberts and Ann Shukman, SCM Press,
used by permission. Extract from *Lenten Triodion* by Kallistos Ware, trs. Mother
Mary and Archimandrite, published by Faber and Faber Ltd. Unattributed
quotations in chapters 8 and 10 are the author's own translation of extracts from
Ilya Basin, *Chtenie Svyashchennogo Pisaniya* [*Reading the Holy Scriptures*], ODSP-SU,
Moscow, 1996.

A catalogue record for this book is available from the British Library

Printed and bound in Great Britain by
Caledonian Book Manufacturing International, Glasgow

CONTENTS

CHAPTER 1

THE BEAUTY OF HOLINESS

NEHEMIAH 9:5

Stand up and bless the Lord your God from everlasting to everlasting. Blessed be your glorious name, which is exalted above all blessing and praise.

Russian Orthodox Christianity is a centuries-old form of worship which still feels very foreign to Western Christians, although many are becoming interested in the deep spirituality of this tradition. The Reformation, which divided Christians, is long in the past. We actively seek fellowship with one another, and this is good, for the Lord Jesus himself prayed on the eve of his sufferings that his followers might be joined together in living unity:

'I ask... also on behalf of those who will believe in me through their word, that they may all be one... I in them and you in me, that they may become completely one, so that the world may know that you have sent me and have loved them even as you have loved me.'

(John 17:20, 21, 23)

The sad story of Christianity is that our churches (which means ourselves) have not only shown ourselves to be unworthy of this love, but there has been hatred and persecution on every side, or, at the very least, simply misunderstandings and silence. So it is good that at last we are beginning to seek ways to build bridges between all our denominations. However, by and large, we are only now beginning to explore and understand Russian Orthodoxy.

'Praise Father, Son and Holy Ghost...':
First steps in understanding Russian Orthodoxy

'Orthodox' means 'true praise'—in Russian it is called *pravoslavie*. That's an exact translation from Greek. In English the word can mean different things—the 'orthodox' way of doing something can mean simply the 'correct' way. An orthodontist is someone who puts your teeth straight! But for the 'dox' bit, think of the doxology: 'Praise God from whom all blessings flow, praise him all creatures here below, praise him above, ye heavenly host, praise Father, Son and Holy Ghost' (Thomas Ken, 1674). And there you have Eastern Orthodox doctrine in a nutshell. Orthodoxy is about worship; it involves all creation, and it is worship of God the Holy Trinity.

So, of course, is all Christian worship. But in the West, since the Reformation, we've often tended to major on doctrine. Churches became places of instruction as much as devotion. People listened to sermons but forgot to fast. We said our prayers but ignored our bodies. Creation got crushed underfoot at the Industrial Revolution. Those 'dark satanic mills' choked the pleasant pastures where, according to the legend, the Lamb of God once was seen. And, yes, all Christian denominations acknowledged the Trinity but, to make a somewhat sweeping generalization, sometimes different denominations emphasized one part of this doctrine more than others. For example, traditionally, Calvinists tended to put more emphasis on God the Father in his awesome majesty, his Divine Providence. Evangelicals fell in love with Jesus, and went abroad as missionaries, or into mines and mills and factories in the Saviour's name. Catholics said their 'Hail Marys' and prayed to the Sacred Heart of Jesus. More recently, the charismatic renewal movement stressed the work and gifts of the Holy Spirit—and brought Catholics and Protestants together after three centuries of mutual suspicion. Vatican II took nuns out of their convents, translated the Mass into the vernacular and encouraged Bible study; we read each other's books and began to realize we weren't so far apart after all. We've still got a long, painful road to travel but Catholics and Protestants are at last beginning to see one another as part of the same Christian family.

For all who are led by the Spirit of God are children of God. For you did not receive a spirit of slavery to fall back into fear, but you have received a spirit of adoption. When we cry, 'Abba, Father!' it is that very Spirit bearing witness with our spirit that we are children of God, and if children, then heirs, heirs of God and joint heirs with Christ—if, in fact, we suffer with him so that we may also be glorified with him.

(Romans 8:14–17)

Orthodoxy, though, is another matter entirely. People holidaying in Greek and Cyprus, who visit Orthodox churches where women are required to wear skirts and headscarves, witness a way of worship which maybe seems just a touch exotic, the sort of thing you associate with warm seas, sunlit vineyards, donkeys and straw hats—but not something to be taken home once the holiday is over.

Moreover, until very recently Russian Orthodoxy remained shut up behind the Iron Curtain. Russian Orthodoxy existed in the West in places like Paris, Brussels and London, mainly for émigrés from post-revolutionary Russia and their descendants. But now there are congregations and churches all over the British Isles: Canterbury, Bath, Exeter, Oxford, Edinburgh, Glasgow, to name just a few places, all have Orthodox churches, using both Greek and Slavonic liturgies. A recent statistic stated that of all the traditional churches in the British Isles the Orthodox Church is the one which is attracting the most new members and showing the greatest growth. I know of at least two Orthodox monasteries in England, another in Wales. Russian-style icons are on sale in many Christian bookshops. Books are published on Orthodox spirituality. Beautiful prayers and litanies from many different Eastern Orthodox traditions are translated into English and greatly enrich our worship.

Orthodoxy is also found in the Far East. Missionary ventures into Siberia in the nineteenth century reached untouched tribes in far eastern Russia and spread to Alaska, which became the centre in the eastern States of America for Orthodox immigrants to America. In 1860 a young monk and missionary hero, Nikolay Kosatkin, served the Russian consulate in Japan as chaplain. His desire, however, was to establish a Japanese Orthodox Church. Texts were translated and the first Japanese Orthodox priests were ordained in 1875; the Orthodox Church numbered more than 35,000 members by the outbreak of World War I. There is now an established metropolitanate of Tokyo and All Japan, whose young people have been leading the way in ecological ventures. A new metropolitanate has been established in Hong Kong. Liturgical texts are being considered for translation into Chinese. In India, worship is conducted in Bengali for the 200-year-old Greek Orthodox community in Calcutta. In Indonesia, Orthodox Christians find their ways of worship bring them closer to the Muslim majority. Orthodox services are held seven times a day, the Muslims pray five times. In the Philippines there are three Orthodox parishes and a convent. There are plans to establish parishes in Thailand and Taiwan. Orthodoxy is African too: it is found in Egypt and Ethiopia, where Orthodox communities stretch back to the earliest years of Christian history, and also in Kenya and Uganda. In Uganda, the Orthodox Church was started by two Anglican Christians who, through their own reading of the Church's history and tradition, decided to become Orthodox, not least because this Church, as well as having its roots in very early times, had not been stained for them by being linked with colonialism and white man's power.

Lebanon, Greece, the Balkans, Bulgaria... all are traditionally Orthodox. There are congregations in Finland and Lithuania and the liturgy is served in those languages too.

Many flames but the light is one:
My personal quest

I am writing about Russian Orthodoxy because that is the form I have come to know and appreciate and, yes, be infuriated with at times. This book is a small tapestry of insights I have gained from my involvement with Russia, which stretches back through all my adult life. I am anxious to represent the Orthodox view to people who, like me, glimpse the profound spirituality of this ancient way, but find it hard to get into. And in Russia this is particularly so because the liturgy is sung and the scriptures are read in a much older form of the language. I hope this book will be a small candle to light the way through the darkness of misunderstanding. The Christian Church is worldwide. If we were all to hold candles, they would all be of different shapes, colours, sizes; our flames would be many, but the light is one.

It's impossible to sum up Orthodoxy in a few words but here's a first attempt: in Orthodoxy, worship is centred on the church building, which is a holy place where, paradoxically, people feel at home. A thirteen-year-old Russian youngster, when asked to describe his way of worship, said, 'Our services last much longer. We don't have any seats. Our churches are much more beautiful than yours and are open all through the week.'

People in Russia ask my husband, an Anglican priest, 'How many services do you hold a week?' They are amazed to learn that church services tend to be held mainly on Sundays and during the rest of the week activities are centred on where people are: at home, in school, in hospital, even in new shopping centres, railway stations and airports.

It's important to remember that for eighty years Russian Orthodoxy had to struggle to survive. Christians of every denomination were discriminated against in Russia. It just wasn't possible to develop a Christian presence in public places or to support any kind of parish life. If a parish priest wanted to visit a sick person in their own home and administer the sacrament, he had to seek official permission from the executive committee of the parish, which was heavily infiltrated by the State. Priests now visit prisons and hospitals; lay-people run centres for orphans and nurse the dying. This is a real spark of light in a country where most people are struggling simply to keep afloat in the tidal wave of a market economy no one was prepared for—an economy which is controlled by the mafia, who developed their networks of collusion in the prison system, and by politicians who are known to be no less corrupt.

Orthodox churches offer believers peace and beauty in the harshness of daily life in Russia, a place to come at all times of the day and pour out sorrow in prayer, to light candles for loved ones and remember the dead. The Orthodox Christians love their

churches and it may be helpful to recall that we too still sometimes sing:

> We love the place, O Lord,
> wherein Thy honour dwells;
> the joy of Thine abode,
> all earthly joy excels.
> It is the house of prayer,
> wherein Thy servants meet;
> and Thou, O Lord, art there,
> Thy chosen flock to greet.

> William Bullock (1798–1874) and
> Henry Williams Baker (1821–77)

Those words bring me, personally, memories of stained glass windows in English village churches, whose stone work dated back
perhaps a thousand years. Doors were open even when there were
no services. Anyone could wander in and look around. I can't
recall seeing anyone kneeling down to pray. You would be a bit
embarrassed to do that, but sometimes an organist would be practising, tucked out of sight in the organ loft in the chancel, and the
sounds would reverberate through the building, a great tidal wave
of beauty which added to the sense of—was it holiness? There was
an aura, certainly, a feeling of something set apart, which made
you want to speak in whispers, to walk slowly, softly, even tiptoe.
Yet there was a feeling too that these old churches were for us to
feel at home in—at least as far as the communion rail.

Those memories come back to me whenever I enter a Russian
Orthodox church. People wander in and out of their open
churches. They are hushed and reverent and do not smile, far less
laugh; if they talk at all it is in whispers but, for all that, they feel
at home. Someone has said Russians are prepared to do anything
in church—except sit down! No one feels constrained, because
everyone is at home. Worship doesn't stop when the long services
finish. The church is a hive of activity, lit by the honeyed light
of votive candles, fragrant with the sweet smell of incense.
Weddings, baptisms, funerals, special prayer for the sick and the

needy—all this is carried on simultaneously in different parts of the church all through the week.

In Glasgow, where I grew up, we sang metrical psalms:

> How lovely is Thy dwelling place,
> O Lord of hosts to me;
> The tabernacles of Thy grace,
> how pleasant, Lord they be!
> ...Behold, the sparrow findeth out
> an house wherein to rest;
> The swallow also for herself
> Hath purchased a nest;
> E'en Thine own altars, where she safe
> her young ones forth may bring,
> O Thou almighty Lord of hosts,
> Who art my God and King.

> (Psalm 84, Scottish Metrical Psalms)

The poetry was memorable, the churches plain. Worship was centred on words, not buildings. 'Who art *my* God and King'—the personal note of devotion was emphasized. And, of course, the great black Bible, borne in by a beadle in morning dress and spread out in its high pulpit where the minister preached, that's what mattered, not the exterior structure, architecture, choir, stained glass or bowing the knee—Heaven forbid! There was a Glasgow street song:

> Piskie, Piskie, Amen!
> Doon on yer knees an up again;
> Presby, Presby, dinnae bend—
> ye'll get to heaven on man's chief end!

Man's chief end being, of course, in the words of the Shorter Catechism, 'to glorify God and enjoy Him for ever'.

Sometimes, greatly daring, I would sneak inside the local Roman Catholic church. It was unlocked, even though it was in a slum clearance area where the police walked in threes and crime was something we took for granted. I would give the holy water stoup a miss and edge into a pew without genuflecting, kneel on the hard ledge which ran the length of the pew and stare at the statues. They seemed a bit garish, not something I felt at home with, but I still kept going along at odd moments. I seldom found anyone there. I think I went to make a statement—to myself, for no one else knew or saw—that the things which unite us matter more than the divisions which so totally (and acrimoniously) separated 'Papes' from 'Proddy dogs' in the Glasgow in which it wasn't safe to walk the streets after a Rangers–Celtic match.

Of Orthodox Christianity I knew absolutely nothing. However, along the road was a Jewish cemetery. The wall was low and if I stood on tiptoe I could see the graves. They stood much closer together than in the rest of the cemetery. The inscriptions were in Hebrew. Fascinated, I stared at the ancient square characters. Once there was a funeral. Of course I looked away, not wanting to stare, but I recall men who stood with covered heads to pray around the grave.

It was probably, then, in connection with Judaism that I first heard the word 'Orthodox'—an Orthodox Jew. But in the 1950s there were news shots of Archbishop Makarios, a Greek Orthodox clergyman who always wore a high black hat with a veil attached. He seemed as exotic and foreign as a Buddhist monk and as a result the term 'Greek Orthodox' hardly seemed to denote anything Christian at all.

Much later on, in my post-student years I chanced upon a Greek Orthodox service in Glasgow. The congregation used a Presbyterian church. People stood cramped between the pews, men on the right, women on the left. Couples separated as they entered church. The service was celebrated at a great distance from us. It was, of course, totally incomprehensible to me. Only one elderly lady went forward to receive communion—and she fainted on her way back, the only bit of visible drama in the long service! I remember thinking what a waste it was, all that effort and only one person communicated! However, afterwards, people (mainly Cypriots who'd come to work in Glasgow) went into the hall for tea. The priest, in his black cassock, moved among us, distributing communion bread—not, he explained, the actual bread offered on the altar, but bread which had been blessed. He was slender and sallow. His long, slim fingers smelled of incense.

I had my first encounter with the Russian Orthodox Church a few months later when I attended a wedding in London. It was a solemn ceremony; the priest wore robes embroidered with gold, and a crown (having to hook his glasses on over its rim—an oddly contemporary note). The couple held long, lighted candles; crowns were held over them as they processed round the church three times, led by the priest. The service was full of pomp and dignity and we, the guests, watched respectfully, but it didn't grab my imagination.

It ought to have done: the priest was Metropolitan Anthony Bloom, whose broadcasts on radio and television, and whose books on prayer, have opened up a whole new dimension of faith for so many in the West.

'The sky is Orthodoxy, the earth is Russia': My first steps on Russian soil

My first experience of Orthodox worship in Russia itself came twenty years after that wedding service.

It was my first ever visit to Russia—or the Union of Soviet Socialist Republics, as our tour guides tartly stressed. My husband Stuart had spent a year in the USSR in the early 1960s, before our marriage. As a loyal Evangelical he seldom attended Orthodox services in that year, but instead went faithfully to the Russian Baptists, where he met a young woman who was already in serious danger because she openly showed herself to be a Christian.

Because of her, we were drawn into praying for Russian Christians and this led us to follow as closely as we could developments 'behind the Iron Curtain'. We read about the work of a Dutch believer, Brother Andrew, who took carloads of Bibles to Russia. We then read the publications of Michael Bourdeaux and Keston College, which was called in those days The Centre for the Study of Religion and Communism. The journal *Religion in Communist Lands* became a focal point for the discussion and understanding of the complex religious situation behind the Iron

Curtain. My horizons widened and I became informed of the struggles of other denominations, including Catholics and Russian Orthodox Christians in the Communist world, for the Bible teaches that we are all part of Christ's body here on earth and 'if one member suffers, all suffer together with it' (1 Corinthians 12:26).

Michael Bourdeaux and his team of research workers not only provide a news service which keeps journalists, churches and politicians accurately informed about religious life in the former USSR, they also publish spiritual literature, a tremendous resource in those closed-off days, and so I began to read writings by Russian Orthodox believers.

The very first issue of the journal *Religion in Communist Lands* carried a fervent and prophetic article which had been smuggled out of Russia. 'It is spring,' the young writer enthused—I quote from memory—'the ice has melted, floods have poured forth all over the Russian land. Rivers are swollen, the torrents of water carry everything away: rubbish of all kinds, yes, and maybe even the river-bank itself. Atheism. The rubbish is atheism, but the sky is Orthodoxy; the earth is Russia. What have atheism and Russia in common? Holy Russia, Orthodox Russia... These words are inextricably linked together. I believe in Orthodoxy and I believe in Russia' (based on 'Notes by a Russian Christian', *RCL* Vol 1, No 1, 1973).

Later, I was to experience for myself the great outpouring of water which is Russian spring. Rivers unlock; water flows; ducks dabble and great floes of ice nudge their way out to sea: every waterway is as congested with sparkling icy cargo as a city ring-road with shining glass and metal at rush hour in summer. Pavements are awash, water cascades from rooftops. Everything sparkles, chuckles and comes alive. The bright blue sky, the bare, unbudded trees are reflected a million times over in myriad floodlets, in the puddles in courtyards, parks and walkways. Spring in Russia, late though it comes, and short-lived though it is, pours out a psalmody of purification and praise.

And exactly that note was sounded in that young man's underground publication which had found its way to Kent.

It would be twenty-five more years before the freeing up would come and the rubbish of atheism would begin to wash away. There was tremendous rejoicing then. Euphoria. But floods contaminate. Raw sewage flows with the flotsam and jetsam. Exactly that is the state of Russia today. In a recent newspaper interview, someone close to President Yeltsin summed up the situation in Russia quite aptly in a recent interview when he said, 'Today's Russia is a state without any organized form of government. Yeltsin doesn't govern, he simply tries to survive physically as well as politically. He is Russia's sickness, not her leader, and every time his own state of health worsens Russia shakes with fever...'.

'I believe in Orthodoxy... I believe in Russia.' Unfortunately, there are the seeds of intolerance here, the sinister sound of fascism. For if Russia is Orthodox, and Orthodoxy is Russian, what place is there for those who follow another creed, even if it is a Christian one? The Russian Orthodox Church leadership is already beginning to impose serious restrictions on other Christian churches. Missionaries have been deported, forward-looking priests have been silenced, books have been burnt. Crude anti-Semitism is openly propagated. The rigid view is that the non-Orthodox are heretics, sectarians, that only Orthodoxy is true—and there are disturbing signs that the leadership, shamefully silent under the Communists, is both bigoted and out of touch with today's world.

'The sons of Communists are becoming Christians'

In that ardent, prophetic article from *Religion in Communist Lands* there were words that I was to carry in my heart for many years, words which were to take my husband and myself back and forth to Russia, until in the end we went there to live and work. 'An amazing thing is happening in Russia,' the author had written; 'the sons of Communists are becoming Christians.'

Sons, and daughters too, the *crème de la crème* of Soviet society, young people with the brightest possible futures even in that shuttered and manacled world. Their parents were professors and scientists. They were students in the most prestigious universities, but they saw through the tired lies of totalitarianism and dropped out. Some chose a hippy lifestyle—as hippy as they could be in the strict controls of a police state; others explored yoga and Eastern mysticism. They read the great Russian thinkers of the nineteenth century, forbidden authors whose books, like the Bible itself, were virtually unobtainable. 'We found our cultural roots rotting in the earth,' said one man, 'and we started to dig them up.'

And for many the path led to faith, to baptism, to disgrace and persecution, but to joy, spiritual joy which was denied them in a regime which boasted that they lived in the best of all possible worlds. The lost sons and daughters came home to God, to Christ, to the disciplines and doctrines of the Church.

'I will get up and go to my father, and I will say to him, "Father, I have sinned against heaven and before you..."' ... But while he was still far off, his father saw him and was filled with compassion; he ran and put his arms around him and kissed him... 'Let us eat and celebrate; for this son of mine was dead and is alive again; he was lost and is found!'

(Luke 15:18, 20, 23–24)

The wonderful painting by Rembrandt, *The Return of the Prodigal*, which hangs in the Hermitage Museum in St Petersburg, took on a special meaning for me in those years: it symbolized the joyful homecoming of so many young Christians who paid for their faith with persecution, prison, psychiatric abuse.

These young Orthodox Christians freely followed the path of suffering which we knew the Baptists had trodden. How could we not think of them as our brothers and sisters too? Their faith illuminated the bleak Russia of Brezhnev's declining years, and the short-lived presidency of the ex-KGB chief, Andropov—who was moribund when he was elected and who died in 1984 when my husband and I were trudging through the snow-bound streets of the two main cities of his mighty empire, visiting Orthodox and Baptist believers.

We went secretly, of course. Secretly and silently. If we spoke at all, it was in Polish. We never took a taxi—foreigners were too obvious. We gave ourselves endless trouble by never revealing to any of our contacts whom else we were trying to see, travelling huge, cold, dark distances among identical housing blocks, carrying bulging bags, pressed for time. Only, of course, to discover later that our friends were all friends of one another, supporting each other in their trials and hardships, sharing books, information, accommodation, prayer, food.

But they appreciated our discretion because even friends can betray.

'Our man in Moscow'

One of the people we met was a lay-reader in one of the few Moscow churches which were still allowed to function in that atheistic state. His job was not to preach but to assist with reading lessons and prayers. He also worked as a caretaker in the church, locking and unlocking the premises, checking the central heating system, making sure everything was in order. He was a man in his mid-thirties, who epitomized everything that is ascetic, other-worldly, unself-seeking in Russian Orthodoxy. I once discussed feminism with him, a hot issue then in British church life. I thought he would totally side with my views but I found myself gently put down: 'Eve sinned first and women bear her blame,' he said, 'but women are given the wonderful example of Mary the Mother of the Lord, of Mary Magdalene, Martha and the many saints. The path of obedience brings lasting fruit...'

And this man certainly lived out the path of obedience in his own life. He turned down the opportunity to become a priest, saying he was unworthy to be anything more than a deacon. He was a living example of all those commands to possess a gentle, forgiving spirit which we find in the Epistles: 'Finally, all of you, have unity of spirit, sympathy, love for one another, a tender heart, and a humble mind. Do not repay evil for evil or abuse for abuse; but, on the contrary, repay with a blessing. It is for this that you were called—that you might inherit a blessing' (1 Peter 3:8–9).

Our friend had served eighteen months in prison for his involvement with an informal group of friends, who formed a Christian seminar which the authorities viciously suppressed. The leaders of this seminar, Russian Orthodox believers, Alexander Ogorodnikov and Vladimir Poresh, who in 1980 had been given maximum sentences of a total of twelve years in prison and exile, became internationally known and, indeed, this lay-reader we were visiting, 'our man in Moscow', made it his ministry to help them and their families. He would later give us news of them from the Gulag.

Seeing his poverty, his simplicity, we wanted to give him some of the provisions we had brought with us. So that evening we went to the church where he worked to meet him, if we could, after the service. It was six o'clock in the depths of Russian winter. I had only been in the city two days but I was already feeling defeated by the harshness of life: the crush of crowds in the Moscow metro, on unheated buses and trams whose windows were frozen so that you couldn't see out. I was depressed by the total conformity. People wore the same drab clothes. No one smiled or laughed. The secret of survival seemed to be to carry a string bag—you might find something to put in it.

'Always winter and never Christmas'

Only the day before, another Russian Orthodox believer, an art historian who had been put into a psychiatric hospital by his parents when, at the age of sixteen, he professed faith in Christ, had summed up his country in an apt comparison. 'Tell us about the Soviet Union,' I had asked this man. 'What is there to tell?' he replied. 'This is the Land of Mordor.' Then he added, with a smile into his greying gold beard, 'You are hobbits!'

He was, of course, referring to Tolkien's epic novel, *The Lord of the Rings*. The Land of Mordor was the land of darkness, 'where the shadows are', where all is observed by one malevolent, all-seeing eye, and hobbits were the little people who blundered in from the Outside World, the Shire. People we visited loved this novel; they typed it out in its entirety and passed it to one another. They loved C.S. Lewis too, his *Narnia* stories, and it seemed to me that I had stumbled into a land which, like Narnia, lay under an evil spell, where, memorably, 'it was always winter and never Christmas' (*The Lion, The Witch and the Wardrobe*, C.S. Lewis, 1950). For, of course, the only public holidays were state ones: The Day of the Soviet Soldier, International Women's Day, The

Day of Victory and, most important of all, May Day and The Day of the Great October Revolution.

On our way to our friend's church we visited an enormous bookshop where all the many titles on sale represented the same official viewpoint. No Tolkien, no C.S. Lewis, nothing you really wanted to read. History was one-sided. The only books about religion rubbished a life of faith. Social problems didn't exist either. Underage crime, for example, was 'hooliganism', an unfortunate aberration which would happily disappear once socialism had eradicated all the degenerate elements in society which still, unfortunately, impeded the glorious forward march of Communism. AIDS was still unknown, but child abuse was—and is still—totally denied. 'It doesn't exist here,' people said, and if I pressed harder and said, 'Oh, but surely…'. 'Well, yes,' they conceded, 'but we don't talk about it.'

My impressions of Russia were that life seemed to have been reduced to an endless, joyless plod along icy pavements where you slithered at your peril. I remember I said breathlessly, grasping hold of Stuart's arm, 'There's no place here for the handicapped, the infirm, the elderly.' Yet Isaiah 58:10 (among many other scriptures) urges upon believers the duty of meeting 'the needs of the afflicted' and I knew that a 24-year-old Russian Orthodox woman, Yelena Sannikova, was in prison at that moment for her protests on behalf of the disabled.

Against this backdrop then, we approached the church.

Worship which makes no apologies for itself

'There it is, that building over there,' Stuart pointed. Falling snow sparkled against the pale light of dim bulbs which barely dispelled the darkness and, hard though I looked, I could see no church at all. We crossed the road. A door opened and a long, thin ray of light spilled out across the dirty, trodden snow. It was like an arrow, showing us where to go, a guiding star, and we followed it gladly. The door shut again, but now I noticed dark shapes of *babushki* (old women) muffled in shawls, bowing, crossing themselves outside.

We pushed open the heavy door, stood within—and saw: brilliance of candlelight, incense and gold, the silent gaze of the icons, the rapt devotion of the worshippers. The church was reasonably full and, as the service proceeded, more and more people came, women and men—by no means only the elderly, even though you could lose a prestigious job, or miss being promoted, if you were noticed.

Since the Industrial Revolution, established churches in the West have largely failed to reach the disadvantaged. Here in Russia, where everyone, except the corrupt leadership, was poor, the church drew in and gave solace to the poorest of the poor.

Unseen choirs sang. The music, the golden warmth, the worship took my breath away. I thought: here the White Witch's spell holds no sway; there is Christmas here, and Easter; there is holiness and space to be. Here is the freedom to hold a different view. If outside is the Land of Mordor, then here is Lothlorien, the Land of the Elves, a place of spiritual healing, where, as in the Isle of Avalon, there 'falls not hail nor any snow', where nothing will hurt nor harm.

Here the handicapped had their place, the elderly came into their own, yes, and the dead and even the demon-possessed. All were present! For as we stood through the long service, which was already underway when we entered, Stuart whispered, 'That looks like a coffin over there—and there's someone inside. A woman, I think.'

I looked across into a side aisle. Laid out on white linen in an open coffin was a woman, her face waxen, lily-like and shrunken in death, receiving before her burial the prayers and blessings of the faithful.

We had come into a service in which there would be the anointing with oil. This was a practice in the early Church: 'Are any among you sick? They should call for the elders of the church and have them pray over them, anointing them with oil in the name of the Lord' (James 5:14). And to this healing service had come a poor tormented soul, a man only in his twenties, bearded and distressed. I didn't look round, but I heard his eldritch moans. 'He's possessed, isn't he? He must be...'.

Stuart nodded. He had the advantage of height. 'He's over there, behind us. He keeps jumping up and down, making the sign of the cross frantically, as though he's trying to drive the demons away.'

Later, people moved forward in a slow, respectful line. 'Is it communion?' I asked.

'No, they're being anointed with oil,' Stuart whispered—he had the second advantage of having studied the Old Slavonic of the service, of which I understood not a word.

The tormented man also moved forward to be anointed. And for almost an hour after the anointing the poor possessed man was at peace. He stood normally, quietly, but then the shouting started again.

After the service no one seemed in a hurry to leave. I wandered around looking at the icons, watching people add yet another slender honey-coloured candle to the many which burned brightly in front of these portrayals of the Lord, his mother, the saints, while Stuart sought out our friend.

He didn't stay long. He didn't want their meeting to be noticed. 'Did you see him?'

'Yes. He said that guy often comes along. But no one here has the gift of exorcism. There's someone in a monastery in Estonia, apparently, who can drive out demons... The anointing helped him though, did you notice? Are you ready? Let's go.'

We gathered up our things. I had taken off my winter coat in the warm church. I had taken my fur hat off too, not knowing the strict rules about keeping heads covered, but no one had given me a telling off, though several old ladies had looked across at me.

I was in a daze. This, my first real experience of Orthodox worship, had been mind-blowing. I felt that I had tasted 'the beauty of holiness' of which the hymn writer sings:

> O worship the Lord in the beauty of holiness,
> Bow down before him, his glory proclaim;
> Gold of obedience and incense of lowliness,
> Bring and adore him, the Lord is his name.

> John Samuel Bewley Monsell, 1811–75

Since then I've lived in Russia. I've attended services in sumptuous cathedrals, in poor, dilapidated churches which had been used as factories or workshops for seventy years... I have prayed with friends in their homes, spoken to priests, monks, nuns. I have taught children from Orthodox families—and been taught by them. My women friends have shown me how their faith spills over into their homes and affects the kind of food they cook at fast or festival. They have taught me prayers in beautiful Old Slavonic, ancient prayers which unite all our Christian traditions. The Lord's Prayer, the thrice repeated Song of the Cherubim, 'Holy God, Holy and Strong, Holy and Immortal, have mercy on us.' The Jesus Prayer, a few simple words which form a whole science of prayer and yet are open to us all: 'Lord Jesus Christ, Son of the Living God, have mercy on me, a sinner' (based on Luke 18:13, 38).

There is much in Russian Orthodoxy which is out of step with today's world. Reform was tentatively suggested before 1917, but then the Russian Orthodox Church was all but wiped out and nothing has moved forward since. The position of women, the rigid, dangerously blinkered role of the hierarchy, the all too close ties between Church and State, the crush and lack of physical comfort endured by lay-people, who hear prayers sung and the Bible read in a language which isn't even Russian, but an earlier form of Slavonic—all these things are called into question by Westerners and by some thinking lay-people in Russia too—and yet, paradoxically, it is this very lack of change which gives Orthodoxy its strength and its attraction.

Once when my husband was in Portugal he was given a present of a 25-year-old port. Its taste was something else, something younger wines just do not have—and especially not the supermarket 'plonk' which is what my palate recognizes. Orthodoxy is a bit like that rich vintage wine. Once you have savoured its worship, you find yourself wanting to know more. I hope that you will stay with me as we explore the riches of this ancient Christian tradition. We are concerned too with what the Russians call 'the Book of Books' and over the years I've become more and more aware just how Bible-based Orthodoxy is. I hope to show how the scriptures are woven into the liturgy and prayers.

Outside St Petersburg stands a church building. Once the parish church of a local Lutheran congregation, it was taken over by the Soviets and turned into a factory. A great metal rod was driven right through it, literally impaling the entire structure. It stands thus today. The congregation have the use of one room and the church remains disfigured, a mute crucifix. And in a sense that's the position of the Bible in Russia. Eighty years of enforced atheism make it hard for ordinary people to believe. They want to. They appreciate the Bible and honour it, but my observation is that the average person does not know, by and large, how to read it, far less apply it to the enormous social and economic problems of Russia today.

The unwise evangelizing of some ill-informed Western missions has made Russian Christians, Orthodox and Baptist, draw back, entrench themselves deeper in their own traditions. Courtesy alone dictates that anyone interested in Russia should learn something of its great religious history. I'm encouraged by the growing interest in Orthodoxy in the West, hoping that we may build bridges across our misunderstandings, appreciate each other and learn from each other. At the moment, it has to be stressed that the official Orthodox hierarchy in Russia unfortunately wants absolutely nothing to do with the non-Orthodox. But there are exceptions, and those who go quietly, humbly and with open hearts will find that the Holy Spirit unites and nourishes us all. We will find that we have much to learn from the Orthodox, whose treasures need no Western advertisement. God can seem too cheaply marketed here; there, God is worshipped, and the worship is costly and makes no apologies for itself: 'Holy God, Holy and Mighty, Holy and Immortal, have mercy on us...'

CHAPTER 2

ONE BODY, MANY PARTS

1 CORINTHIANS 12:12-13

*For just as the body is one and has many members, and all the
members of the body, though many, are one body, so it is with
Christ. For in the one Spirit we were all baptized into one
body—Jews or Greeks, slaves or free—and we were all made to
drink of one Spirit.*

The Eastern Orthodox theologian, Kallistos Ware, has written of
the twentieth century: 'It is a century of which it has been said,
"It is by no means impossible that in the thirty years between
1918 and 1948 more Christians died for their faith than in the
first 300 years after the crucifixion."'

In fact, as far as Russia is concerned we can safely add on
another forty years of Christian suffering, imprisonment, slave
labour, even deaths. The Gulag began to release its dissident prisoners in any meaningful way only after 1986. In 1988, however,
Soviet Russia, whose official religion was still atheism, acknowledged publicly that it was now a thousand years since the kingdom we now know as Russia officially embraced Christianity. The
Soviet State, which for the past seventy years had forced its citizens
to believe there is no God, was obliged to celebrate a thousand
years of Christianity, and it was a heady time, with people flocking
openly to church. However, even as the official celebrations were
going on, with all the pomp and ceremony of which Russia—and
Orthodoxy—are capable, people of faith—Christians and Jews
were still in prison.

---

*Remember those who are in prison,
as though you were in prison with them...* (Hebrews 13:3)

Right from the earliest years of the revolution, Orthodox
Christians suffered in the Gulag. Their faith and endurance was
less talked about in the West than the faith of the Evangelical

Baptists. We even asked, 'Can the Orthodox be Christians?' And we learned that they could!

In the last chapter, I shared how my path towards appreciation of Orthodoxy was a gradual one in which the story of individual believers played an important part. Having only minimally experienced Orthodox worship, knowing nothing of its offices, its liturgy, its life, I read in the journals of Keston College about, for example, the prayer experience of Anatoly Levitin, an elderly Orthodox layman whose celebrated 'at homes' used to see the cream of the Moscow intelligentsia crowding into his tiny room in a tumbledown shack outside the city. They had to catch an overcrowded electric train with hard wooden seats, travel for about twenty minutes and then trek along narrow, muddy country lanes for about another forty minutes until they came upon a ramshackle little house. One room, not much bigger than a cupboard, was occupied by Anatoly Emmanuilovich Levitin. On his 'open' days he would be surrounded by young people. Friends rushed out to the nearest shop to buy sardines, bread, sugar, butter. As people gathered they would find one of the young people washing potatoes which were boiled with an onion. Tea, that great stand-by of Russian life, was served in chipped glass tumblers. Soon the room filled with smoke and lengthy arguments. There were believers and atheists, for here, an oasis in the great desert of conformity, people could talk and argue about whatever they liked.

Anatoly's 'receptions' were noted by the KGB. Agents tailed the visitors, spied on the gatherings and this elderly man served two periods in prison in the 1960s and again in 1971. The prophet Isaiah assures us: 'Even youths will faint and be weary, and the young will fall exhausted; but those who wait for the Lord shall renew their strength...' (Isaiah 40:30–31). This was the experience of Anatoly Levitin, who testified from prison:

The greatest miracle of all is prayer. I have only to turn my thoughts to God and I suddenly feel a strength which bursts into me from somewhere, bursts into my soul, into my entire being. What is it? Psychotherapy? No, it is not psychotherapy, for where would I, an insignificant, tired old man, get this strength which renews me and saves me, lifting

*me above the earth? It comes from without and there is no force on earth
that can even understand it...*

*The basis of my life is the Orthodox liturgy (I do not, of course, deny
other forms). Therefore, while in prison I attended the liturgy every day
in my imagination. At 8 am I would begin walking around my cell, re-
peating to myself the words of the liturgy. At that moment I felt myself
inseparably linked with the whole Christian world and then, standing before the face of the Lord and feeling almost physically his wounded and
bleeding body, I would begin praying in my own words... The prison
walls moved apart and the whole universe became my residence, visible
and invisible, the universe for which that wounded, pierced body offered
itself as a sacrifice... Not only my prayer, but much more the prayer of
many faithful Christians helped me. I felt it continually. It worked from
a distance, lifting me up as though on wings, giving me living water and
the bread of life, peace of soul, rest and love.*

RCL, Vol 2, No 2, March–April 1974, slightly abridged

It's important to recall that in the totalitarian state committed to
socialist realism, talk of 'a force without' which 'lifts you on
wings...' was enough to commit someone to psychiatric hospital
and mood-changing drugs. Indeed, it was said in the 1970s that
a mental hospital was the only proper place for people deluded
enough to believe in God. Baptist and Orthodox believers, including monks and nuns, were injected with neuroleptic drugs, which
destroyed them physically as well as mentally. Stuart and I know
someone who cannot live fully as a mature adult because of enforced drug abuse. Moreover, that beautiful piece of writing on
prayer was written in a cramped prison cell in the depths of Soviet
Asia, in soaring summer temperatures and cruel conditions. At one
point Anatoly shared his cell with two murderers. One had lived
in what was still Soviet Lithuania and had gone into a church and
seen 'the twisted body of a man hanging on two pieces of wood'.
Like many, many Soviet citizens he had no idea who Jesus is.

As I read of the faith of this man who had been a headmaster
but who was, of course, sacked once he started writing Christian
articles and going openly to church; of the path to faith of
Alexander Ogorodnikov and Vladimir Poresh; of the Christian

poet Irina Ratushinskaya, who at twenty-nine was sentenced to a stringent thirteen years' imprisonment, and many others, I could only say that they are my brothers and sisters in Christ. Like many other Western Christians, my husband and I prayed and campaigned on behalf of these imprisoned believers. How could we think that because they followed a different tradition, one we knew so little about, they were any less Christian than ourselves? Would we have dared as much, sacrificed so much? Alexander Ogorodnikov, of the Moscow Christian Seminar, had the bitter experience of being denounced by his wife, who divorced him because he had chosen to suffer for Christ. (She would have been put under enormous pressure to do so. Another believer, a Baptist, told me only recently how the KGB so often found out a person's weaknesses and played on these.)

'We had nothing but love': Vladimir and Tatiana's story

Alexander Ogorodnikov's friend and fellow member of the Seminar, Vladimir Poresh, was repeatedly denied visits from his wife, Tatiana. She travelled the vast distances to meet him on the twice-yearly visits prisoners were officially allowed, only to be turned away at the prison gates. They had two meetings in six years. She was expecting their second child when her husband was arrested. Both daughters drew pictures for 'Papa' in prison, little girls growing up without their father. But growing up with faith in Christ, knowing prayers and Bible stories from their earliest years.

Tatiana recalls the time before Vladimir's arrest with tears. 'We were poorer than poor,' she relates. 'We had nothing, but we had love.'

Tatiana was referring to the love of friends like the lay-reader my husband and I had met in Moscow, and others who were ready to risk their freedom for the sake of the gospel. 'We know love by this, that he laid down his life for us—and we ought to lay down our lives for one another' (1 John 3:16). These young people took that verse literally and made self-sacrifice the hallmark of their lives, but the Epistle continues: 'How does God's love abide in anyone who has the world's goods and sees a brother or sister in need and yet refuses help?' Tatiana and Vladimir had also entered a community of faith, believers worldwide whom they didn't know, but who prayed for them, who lit candles of hope at a very dark time, wrote letters to prisoners, sent gifts, support. The Iron Curtain almost totally cut off Eastern Europe from its Western neighbours. Almost—but not quite.

'Ask, and it will be given you,' said Jesus, 'search, and you will find; knock, and the door will be opened for you' (Matthew 7:7). Prayer crossed that closed frontier. Prayer opened prison doors. Remember those heady days in Poland, when dockers knelt in puddles to receive communion openly in their place of work? Remember the great surge of joy when Cardinal Karol Wojtyla, Archbishop of Krakow, became Pope? Russian Orthodox Christians, struggling in un-freedom, were overjoyed. What did it matter that this man came from another denomination, another language? This new Pope was a brother Slav and a brother Christian. A great unstoppable thaw was beginning and the ice was starting to crack. And when the Berlin Wall finally came tumbling down, we knew it had been toppled by prayer, and we rejoiced in the huge bonfire of freedom which had been fed by all those individual flickering flames, small candles of hope.

But that was way in the future. Yet Tatiana and Vladimir, in the late 1970s, took candles of hope into their own hands and made their marriage vows not in a Soviet Palace of Weddings, a State registry office, among smiles and congratulations, but in church—a thing unheard of in those days. 'They can't be Russians; they must be foreign,' Tatiana had overheard the old women whisper in disbelief.

But no, they were Russians, a young couple who had chosen the disgrace of a church wedding. The Lord Jesus, on the eve of his path of suffering and death, reminded his disciples, 'Remember the word that I said to you, "Servants are not greater than their master." If they persecuted me, they will persecute you' (John 15:20). Soon Vladimir was being hunted from pillar to post, beaten up as he travelled on the underground trains; he had his glasses snatched from him, was insulted, kicked and finally arrested and put on trial—a trial which was a celebration of resurrection joy. Vladimir testified, not without irony:

I am proud that I belong to our Russian Orthodox Soviet Church, soaked in the blood of more martyrs than the whole of Christianity has seen, and I am glad it is a church that young people are joining... I am a Christian and my world-view, based on Christianity and the Church, includes the world in all its fullness... You have seen the witnesses... I saw joy on their faces... this hall was filled with a constant sense of joy, even though I am in custody. This is a new religious community; these are warriors for the Church of Christ, conquering the whole world for her. It is my friends who are Christ's warriors, who will conquer the world for him. This new spiritual reality, this communal Christian view of the world, is being created everywhere, even here in the courtroom, and here I see the goal and meaning of this trial...

RCL, *Vol 10, No 3, 1982*

Tatiana recalls that it was like Easter. Joy flowed out into the unwelcoming ante-rooms and corridors of the court. Friends kissed, embraced. They celebrated Vladimir's savage sentence with flowers and applause. 'Christ is risen! He is risen indeed!' The great Easter acclamation rang through the Soviet courtroom.

---

*Then the king gave the command, and Daniel was...
thrown into the den of lions.* (Daniel 6:16)

Much later, after Vladimir's release, Tatiana and her two younger children came to stay with us in Scotland. Her little boys were both under three. They had been born when their father, thin as a concentration camp victim, had returned home to an overcrowded flat to do hard manual work as an assistant to a housepainter—all that was open to him with his criminal record. The children came across a picture Bible story of Daniel in the lions' den (Daniel 6:10–23). My Russian was still very limited—and theirs was too! I said, 'Your Papa was like Daniel.' And I saw the eyes of the elder boy light up with recognition—and thereafter he took the book to bed with him and carried it around wherever he went.

Tatiana and her two little boys stayed with us at a very difficult period of our lives—but the joy they brought us was truly heavenly. And they were welcomed everywhere with such love that divisions of denomination made no difference at all!

It so happened that while Tatiana was staying with us a documentary film was shown on television. It had been made by a French television team who visited the very prison in which Vladimir had been held. We saw the prisoners look wide-eyed with total disbelief when they realized that these really were foreign cameramen and journalists, who were showing the world their plight. Tatiana sat riveted to the screen. 'Look at him,' she kept saying, whenever the camp commandant was shown. 'Look at that face! Not a flicker of humanity. No compassion. Can you imagine asking him to please allow me to see my husband? And being turned away every time.'

Her first meeting with her husband, five years after his imprisonment, sounded like something straight out of the pages of a novel by Tolstoy. She had travelled three days and nights to the dump of a place where the prison camp was. She had at once sought an interview with the commandant, but, as usual had been refused. She had spent the night in an appalling hostel and now, at eight o'clock in the morning, was on her way to prison to beg to be allowed to see Vladimir.

'Do not worry about anything,' counsels the apostle Paul, 'but in everything by prayer and supplication with thanksgiving let your requests be made known to God.' Tatiana, whose life as a wife and mother has been one long struggle against almost unendurable odds, knows the meaning of Philippians 4:6 better than most, and that dull morning her prayers were answered.

'The road was blocked,' she recalled. 'Someone said, "The prisoners are coming." It was a grey day; a drizzly rain was falling and, right enough, along came rank after rank of prisoners in their camp uniforms being marched along to work. I kept watching—they all looked so alike, so thin. Would I be able to see Vladimir—even to recognize him after so long? And suddenly, there he was! He was wearing a funny sort of cap. He caught sight of me, smiled and raised his cap. I waved to him. And that was it. Our first meeting. We hadn't even been able to speak! But, amazingly, for the first time ever, the commandant grudgingly allowed me in to see him.'

Both Vladimir's daughters, at different times over the last ten years, have told me their experience of their first meeting with their father. 'I was so excited,' recalled the older girl. 'Going to see Papa! I thought we'd sit and drink tea together. But we were kept in separate rooms. We could see each other through a glass screen. We had to talk to one another by phone.'

It was the same for her sister. She was six and had gone with her paternal grandfather, a respected academic who had been demoted when his son had been sent to prison. They had travelled all the way to the region where her father was being held, the father she had never seen. 'I just said, "Papa! Papa!" I wanted to run right up to him and give him a hug, but we were separated by that screen. But the guard on duty was a woman and when it was time to go she said, "I shouldn't do this, but I'll let you in to see your father." And I ran right up to him and he took me on his knee.'

The girls are beautiful young women now. The elder married recently. She stood regally in her borrowed wedding dress beneath the nuptial crown, and her little brothers followed the procession, solemnly holding the train, all of them moving with devotion and grace through the complicated wedding ceremony. Watching, I thought, this is Orthodoxy's gift to the young couple, this mystical, courtly service, the rich singing of the unaccompanied voices of the choir. Whatever lies ahead for the bridal pair, for these moments at the start of their marriage they are more than just bride and groom—they are prince and princess, honoured in the courts of heaven.

This sense of the sublime, of the presence of 'angels and archangels and all the company of heaven', this is the garment of praise with which Russian Orthodoxy splendidly envelops its own. It is no easy faith. The young couple and their attendants, who held the heavy crowns above their heads, were required to fast, for they would receive communion once the promises were made…

Father Gheorge Calciu

Remember… those who are being tortured,
as though you yourselves were being tortured. (Hebrews 13:3)

In those early years when I had prayed for prisoners whose names I could hardly pronounce, I had no idea that I would have the privilege of meeting them and their friends. But, in a very real way, their faith, their writings made them my first tutors in the ways of Eastern Orthodoxy, and so, indelibly, was the Rumanian Orthodox priest Father Gheorge Calciu.

Most of us strive after holiness, but in the frenetic rush of living, in the pain and turmoil of life, prayer often seems to hit no higher than the ceiling; our hearts too seldom seem to be centred within, where we may hear 'the still small voice' which speaks not in the fire, nor in the wind but 'in a sound of sheer silence' (1 Kings 19:12). Father Calciu seemed shot through with holiness: years of solitary confinement which he endured as a Christian had chiselled deep veins of love in his heart. Of him it might be said, as Metropolitan Anthony Bloom wrote of a young believer who had also suffered years in prison, 'They have burnt out everything. Only love remains' (*Living Prayer*, Anthony Bloom, 1966).

Here is Father Gheorge's story. After World War II, the Communists took over Bucharest and, as a young medical student of twenty, Gheorge took part in a demonstration against the new atheistic regime. The apostle Peter, arrested in Jerusalem for civil disobedience declared, 'We must obey God, rather than any human authority' (Acts 5:29). Gheorge did no less. He was arrested and put in prison, not to emerge for another fifteen years. The prison in which he was held was so horrendous that few people survived. Gheorge saw men go mad, break under torture. He had no contact with the outside world. His own mother didn't know if he was dead or alive.

He was thirty-five years of age when he was released and, like the psalmist, he could say, 'From the horns of the wild oxen you have rescued me. I will tell of your name to my brothers and sisters; in the midst of the congregation I will praise you: You who fear the Lord, praise him!' (Psalm 22:21–23) So, as a thank-offering to God that he was still alive, he became a priest. There was a slight free-ing up in Rumania at this time. But once he was ordained he was appointed to a teaching post in French and New Testament stud-ies at the Orthodox seminary in Bucharest, where he soon fell foul of the authorities once more. His lectures and sermons were so popular that the university authorities locked the students in their rooms to prevent them flocking to hear a man who denounced atheism as a 'philosophy of despair': 'Fools say in their hearts, "There is no God." They are corrupt, they do abominable deeds… They have all gone astray, they are all alike perverse; there is no one who does good, no not one' (Psalm 14:1, 3). The psalm continues, 'Have they no knowledge, all the evildoers who eat up my people as they eat bread, and do not call upon the Lord?' Those words are an apt description of the leadership of Rumania of the day and of the suffering of the people and in his lectures Father Gheorge spoke openly about the problems of the enslaved Church.

'The more they beat me, the more I had to pray…'

Father Gheorge was arrested again in March 1979 and suffered beatings and ill-treatment. In July of that year he was sentenced to ten years in prison. He was married with a son. (If clergy in Eastern Orthodoxy are married before ordination, they are allowed to remain so. They may not marry after ordination and bishops are drawn only from the ranks of the celibate. Married priests serve in parishes.)

Once when Mrs Calciu came to visit her husband she saw that his fingers were broken—the police had beaten him because he had lifted his hands to make the sign of the cross and pray.

'I knew what they would do to me, but it was almost as if some force stronger than I—and far stronger than a whole army of tor-turers—was pulling my hands up on invisible strings. The more they beat me, the more I had to keep on praying,' Father Gheorge later recalled.

The regime were plainly out to rid themselves of this trouble-some priest! But he had challenging words for the West as well:

'You were enthusiastic to see man put his feet on the moon but you do not know how to plead for your brothers. We have been chosen for captivity and suffering… but we want you to feel for us in our suffering and cry out when we cannot: Enough!'

Father Calciu was frequently put into punishment cells, where the totally inadequate diet of normal prison life was reduced to starvation, freezing conditions and constant surveillance. A prisoner was given food only one day in three. His—or her—bed was a board which folded out from the wall and had to be shut away from 6 am until 6 pm, so there was nowhere to sit or rest.

The underground cells were freezing, the floors running with water, infested with mice. Irina Ratushinskaya, who was also kept in such cells for the slightest supposed infringement of prison regulations (which a prisoner was never shown), wrote a memorable poem about a little mouse who came to visit her in her solitary confinement.

Alexander Ogorodnikov, too, wrote of the 'refined and calculated cruelty' of this regime which, little by little, was making him lose his sight. Another famous prisoner, Nathan Sharansky, who embraced the Jewish faith of his fathers, endured three years underground, where he did indeed become blind. In his autobiography he narrates how his fellow prisoner, Vladimir Poresh, would read the psalms to him, for he could no longer see.

The spiritual suffering was even more devastating than the physical torture. But Father Gheorge relates movingly how once he was kept in the punishment cells on Easter Day. He longed for a piece of bread with which to celebrate holy communion, but it was a day without food. He had water, which could represent wine, but no bread. An inner voice told him to knock at the door and ask the guard for bread. But the guard on duty was a particularly brutal man who always insulted Father Calciu, shouting obscenities at him, beating him up, bullying him. However the inner voice refused to be silent and in the end, greatly fearing, Father Gheorge knocked at the cell door and asked for a small piece of bread with which to celebrate his Easter communion.

The guard swore and cursed and slammed the door leaving Father Gheorge alone and deeply sorrowful that he had asked for bread.

Suddenly, the key turned in the lock. The door opened and the guard silently handed in a large piece of bread—and after that this man never beat up or insulted Father Calciu again, so that he was soon removed from duty along that corridor for not being cruel enough.

But Father Gheorge, full of praise and thanksgiving, celebrated communion in his cell. 'And that Easter I felt myself to be in Paradise,' he said.

'People of Rumania, look what they do to your priest!'

Campaigners in the West—and Ceausescu's desire to win economic support—saved Father Gheorge from the slow death which was being dealt out to him. But he had no idea of this. One day his cell was opened. He was blindfolded and bundled out to a car. The windows were completely blackened. Guards with loaded pistols sat on either side of them—he felt the pistols they kept pointed at his head.

'They told me they were taking me away to kill me,' he said. They drove for many hours, so that he lost all sense of time and place. Then they stopped and hustled him outside. He felt the fresh air, felt himself being pushed along, tried to prepare himself for the death they had ready for him, when suddenly his blindfolds were taken off and he found himself at his own home.

He had been set free. But police guarded his house day and night. When he and his wife went out to market they were surrounded by six armed policemen, two in front, two behind and one at either side. Adriana Calciu, a retiring woman who never thought to raise her voice in public, had learnt to be fearless in her husband's defence. 'People of Rumania,' she would call out, 'look what they do to your priest.'

Soon afterwards, Father Calciu, his wife and 20-year-old son were thrown out of their homeland for ever.

Not tall, still handsome, in his sixties with a neat beard and a fine head of white hair, Father Gheorge and Adriana, struggling with limited English (he speaks French fluently; she knows German), struggling too with a different diet, particularly difficult for them at times of the Orthodox fasts, would tour the United States of

America and Western Europe, speaking in churches, working tirelessly on behalf of religious freedom in their tortured land.

And, despite this exhausting programme, Father Gheorge would fast totally on Wednesdays and Fridays. These are days in Orthodoxy, as they used to be in Western Christianity, when diet is spare, fish is allowed, but no meat—this is an ascetic fast. However, there is also the concept of total fast, and Father Calciu ate and drank nothing all day, from sundown the previous evening. He did this, he explained, because of a vow he had made in prison, that if he survived, he would fast and pray for all prisoners and captives and particularly those in his own homeland.

I used to wonder, what keeps him going? He and his wife would arrrive at our home at about 4 pm, having been driven from an airport, or from a train, or from a meeting in some other place. I would make tea, but Father Gheorge would take nothing. He should have been able to break his fast at 6 or 7 pm, but there would be no time. He had to go out to an evening meeting. He would speak of his experiences in prison, greet total strangers, giving, giving of himself—and something radiant would shine out of him. Watching him, I understood that 'if the Son makes you free, you will be free indeed' (John 8:36).

What a feast of joy we would have later that evening, for other friends would gather wherever Father Gheorge went. I understood the meaning of the scripture: 'Do not neglect to show hospitality to strangers, for by doing that some have entertained angels without knowing it' (Hebews 13:2). But Father Gheorge was no stranger—for the circles of love and prayer are endless, and know no division of doctrine or language.

This is something the Russian Orthodox Church in freedom has, by and large, still to realize. Once, when I was teaching the Bible in a school in St Petersburg, I wrote confidently on the board: 'All one in Christ Jesus' (Galatians 3:28). At once a hand shot up. A round-faced wee boy, a staunch defender of the faith, said, 'No! *Batyushka* doesn't allow this.'

Batyushka is an old Russian word reserved for priests; it's both respectful and intimate. But *Batyushka*'s word for the faithful is law. This wee boy adhered to the strict tenets of Orthodoxy, and he was all of ten. Because the school kitchen didn't observe a non-meat diet, he—and other children—brought black bread to school with them all through Lent and Advent and had no hot food all day.

I showed the class a photograph of a cage protest on behalf of the Christian prisoner Irina Ratushinskaya. My young pupil didn't want to budge his position. 'She can't have been really Orthodox,' he said.

'Oh, yes she is!' I assured him, but I saw in his eyes that he was far from convinced. Only the Orthodox are true.

'Catholics deviated from the truth a thousand years ago,' one woman, a guest in our home in Edinburgh, told me. 'And as for Protestants, their position is simply to be in opposition.' (Opposed to the truth of the Church, as handed down by the Councils and the Fathers, she meant.) 'In fact,' she went on, 'to be Protestant is the first step to becoming atheist.'

So while Western Christians try to explain to the Russian Orthodox Christians that there are important lessons to be learned from our experience of the Reformation, the Orthodox view is that it is we who have deviated from the truth, and our reformed faith is a real barrier for them. The Russian Orthodox neither understand nor seek pluralism. The view is that only Orthodoxy contains the fullness of God's grace. 'A Christian without the church is like a fish out of water,' wrote Father John of Kronstadt at the beginning of the century: only Orthodoxy can feed the soul with spiritual food—and cast out the powers of darkness and minister to the diseased. The holy Church bears and ministers the Spirit of Christ to the world—and for the Orthodox this means the truth enshrined in tradition. The Apostle Paul writes in Ephesians 1: 'God put... all things under Christ's feet and gave him to the church as supreme Lord over all things. The church is Christ's body, the completion of him who himself completes all things everywhere' (vv. 20, 22, GNB). And this is what Orthodoxy embodies. 'We are always and everywhere together as the Body of Christ on earth, as in heaven,' the Orthodox say. 'Our worship is an uninterrupted continuity from the earliest centuries of our Christian era till now.'

So the barriers between us are huge. Those, like Vladimir Poresh and Father Gheorge Calciu, who see beyond the divisions, are in the minority. And, in their own way, Russian Evangelical Baptists are as unyielding as the Orthodox Christians. People all over the former Soviet Union, cut off for so long from communication with the outside world, are largely uninformed about our churches. 'Do you have holy communion in your church?' I'm asked. 'Do you have baptism?' *Are you even Christian?* Yet as we learn about one another's traditions, we light flickering flames of hope. And maybe the walls of division will tumble down once more.

Chapter 3

How Lovely is
Your Dwelling Place

Psalm 26:8

*O Lord, I love the house in which you dwell,
and the place where your glory abides.*

In AD410 the unthinkable happened: pagan tribes sacked the centre of civilization, Rome. People feared the imminent end of the world. But by then Christianity had become the state religion of the whole Roman Empire, and although much was destroyed in the ravage and plunder of that time, on the far edges of Europe, Eastern and Western, a light still shone. Candles of faith and hope burst into flame—and their light has never gone out. St Martin of Tours in Gaul, St Ninian in Galloway, St Patrick in Ireland—whose life takes in the troubled fifth century—and, a hundred years later, St Columba in Iona, toiled on the borders of the known world and flung a great net of missionary and educational influence out over the ruins of the mighty Roman Empire, successfully drawing in the Frankish and Germanic tribes which had overrun Western Europe. In time this Christian influence spread east of the Rhine and down to the Danube, taking in the Hungarians and Western Slavs.

But in the century before the collapse of Rome, in the deserts of Egypt, Syria and Palestine, the cradle of Christianity, a light of gentleness, austerity, and what seems to Western minds near madness, also shone. It, too, has never been extinguished.

The song of the desert

Men and women 'dropped out' of society and went out into the desert. They were subversives, radicals—not, however, because they had a programme to follow, a doctrine of political or social reform. Far from it! Their desire was for the kingdom of God. If they were silent, it was because they were listening to God. Cut off from the sound of human voices, they heard the voice of creation: the desert sang to them of God.

'The wilderness and the dry land shall be glad, the desert shall rejoice and blossom; like the crocus it shall blossom abundantly, and rejoice with joy and singing' (Isaiah 35:1–2). In those years, three, four, five hundred years after the birth of Christ, the desert indeed seemed to blossom with the joy and the fullness of the Holy Spirit. Russian Orthodoxy has directly inherited this tradition, and the Orthodox are interested to learn that the life of the Desert Fathers has influenced Western Christianity too. Martin of Tours imbibed it and passed its teachings to Ninian, who brought Christianity to Galloway and established a centre of spiritual power which spread out all over Scotland, perhaps as far away as the Shetland Isles. People still make pilgrimages to the cave where, it is said, Ninian prayed, retreating from the halls of power to follow the way of the desert.

Celtic Christianity is close to it: gentle Cuthbert standing all night up to his neck in the cold North Sea reciting the Psalter was following, in his own way, the tradition of the desert. So were his monks. The story goes that the douce brothers, the monks of Lindisfarne, once returned to their cells to find their straw pallets occupied by eider ducks. They gave their beds to the birds and slept on the earthen floor until the ducklings were hatched. Or there is St Kevin who, lost in prayer, failed to notice that a blackbird had started to weave her nest on his outstretched palm. Kevin kept his hand raised until the young were hatched and flown. Lovely, even if sometimes unlikely, stories abound and they carry us eastwards to Italy and forward in time to the *Little Flowers* of St Francis, and eastwards again to the forests of Russia, where holy St Sergius shared his supper with a bear. And forward in time to our own age, for people who are both subversive and sane still choose to live as hermits.

When people hone themselves to the very edges of existence it often seems to be that the human spirit, illumined by the Holy Spirit, achieves the primeval harmony which creation lost when Adam sinned. 'The wolf shall live with the lamb, the leopard shall lie down with the kid, the calf and the lion and the fatling together, and a little child shall lead them' (Isaiah 11:6). The desert seems to bring fruitfulness out of austerity, just as Samson found honey in the jaws of the lion he had killed (Judges 14:8, 9).

The writings gathered by disciples of the Desert Fathers (and Mothers), which distilled the wisdom of the wilderness, the cutting edge of prayer whose core is love, are a vital source of Orthodox spirituality, which now inspire many people in the West. This ancient way has become once again—in our own day of multi-national conglomerates, which are networked by instant electronic information—a drawing power and unifying force. People who mine its spiritual treasures often also go on to explore the traditions of Eastern Orthodoxy.

The Spirit brings freedom—but churches need rules

All things should be done decently and in order.
(1 Corinthians 14:40)

The desert is a harsh environment, which parches rather than sustains; though, paradoxically, it is a well-spring of prayer, fertile soil for the nurture of the spirit. The desert is marginal and minimalist —but churches have to be structured. The very earliest Christian communities needed rules—as we see from the Acts of the Apostles and the Epistles, and although they originally met in peoples' homes, they soon needed buildings. To maintain buildings you need labour and capital; you need political and social stability. The churches, too, needed leadership and very early in the Acts of the Apostles we read:

The twelve called together the whole community of disciples and said, 'It is not right that we should neglect the word of God in order to wait on tables. Therefore, friends, select from among yourselves seven men of good standing, full of the Spirit and of wisdom, whom we may appoint to this task, while we, for our part, will devote ourselves to prayer and to serving the word.' What they said pleased the whole community...

(Acts 6:2–5)

The first church council was held in Jerusalem, presided over by Peter and James, the brother of the Lord (Acts 15:6–29). The principle of *sobornost*, gathering together in council, is still the basis of Orthodoxy. In the centuries following the meeting of the council recorded in Acts 15, other major church councils were held, in which the leadership thrashed out doctrines which Western and Eastern churches still acknowledge—the Nicene Creed, for instance—but by the time the Council of Nicea was held in AD325 serious rifts had already developed between East and West.

The centre of Eastern Christianity was, of course, Constantinople, the city founded by Emperor Constantine, who modestly gave it his name. Constantine, too, was the emperor who made Christianity the official religion of the Roman Empire; he saw the cross shining in the stars on the eve of battle, along with the words, 'By this sign you shall conquer.'

So while the hermits were seeking salvation in the desert, the Christian Church was being richly endowed by emperors and empresses who went regally on pilgrimage to Jerusalem. The Pope may reign in Rome, but in the East the churches are governed by patriarchs who meet in council: Jerusalem, Antioch, Alexandria and Constantinople are the ancient patriarchates of Eastern Orthodoxy. The question of power, as much as difference in doctrine, divided East and West then as now.

Jesus himself pointed out the contrasts between the desert and the centres of political power: 'What did you go out into the wilderness to look at? A reed shaken by the wind? What then did you go out to see? Someone dressed in soft robes? Look, those who wear soft robes are in royal palaces' (Matthew 11:7, 8).

These words have come to my mind more than once as I've stood through the long hours of an Orthodox service. Paradoxically, however, for all its pomp and ceremony, Orthodoxy hasn't forgotten the spirituality of the desert. The hermit monks of Orthodoxy, filled with spiritual gifts, have a profound influence in their Church. Moreover, the basis of the Orthodox Church is not preaching but worship. The liturgical day begins 'at even when the sun was set' (Henry Twells, 1868), with evening prayer. The liturgy is also served in the morning, and at other times of the day at fast or festival, and undergirding the visible worship of the

Orthodox Church is the more hidden life of the monastery, where prayer is offered regularly throughout the twenty-four hours of each day. At a deeper level still for every believer there is the life of continual prayer based on the simple words of the Jesus Prayer.

Russia has been in the terrible desert of atheism, which destroyed churches and threw holy things out into the mud, severely curtailing the activity of every church. All too often the price of survival was servile compliance with a cynical regime, and that was a very real desert indeed. But when we enter an Orthodox church and witness the splendid ceremonies, the sheen of gold everywhere, even in the vestments worn by the priests, we know we are watching—and perhaps also, for all its foreignness, participating in—a form of worship which takes us right back through the long story of Christianity, something which is ancient and yet from which we may draw new strength for today. Its opulence may sometimes repel. Its priests, who process out from behind the iconostasis which separates them from the people, chant in bass voices so deep they shock; these men with flowing beards may seem too remote from our modern world, too fat... I often wonder: how do they pass the time behind their elaborate screen, the Royal Doors? Crude anti-clerical propaganda showed them tearing into haunches of meat and quaffing wine. This is vile but, it has to be said, their very apartness lent itself to such conjecture.

Baptism of Russia—AD988

And yet there is a purity of worship and prayer which reminds me that in AD988 Vladimir of Russia (he ruled from AD980 to 1015) is said to have chosen Orthodoxy for its beauty. And beauty has unashamedly been the hallmark of Orthodoxy ever since. Of course paganism didn't die out immediately once the Emperor had decreed that his people should be baptized. The god of thunder was still worshipped; so were many gods of trees and rivers and lakes. But in the city of Kiev, now the capital of the Ukraine, a rich civilization was beginning, which looked to Byzantium for its inspiration. The country which became Christian Russia—indeed, Holy Russia—was first known as *Kievan Rus*.

Neighbouring Poland had embraced Christianity in AD966 and

chose the Roman form, which would keep Poland firmly rooted in Western Europe through all the vicissitudes of its often tragic history. A century earlier, however, another group of Slavs had enjoyed a period of stability as a nation. This was Greater Moravia, now the eastern part of the Czech Republic. It was soon to collapse under attacks by the nomadic tribes of Hungary, but in its heyday the Prince, Rostislav, wanting a buffer against the political influence of powerful German clergy, sought missionaries from among Slav settlers in Thessalonika, Greek Orthodox monks who knew Slavonic. Their influence was to prove longer lasting than the state of Prince Rostislav itself, for the monks brought Orthodoxy into the heart of what we now call Europe and put the Slav languages into writing; one of these first missionaries, St Constantine-Cyril, gave his name to the Cyrillic alphabets of Russia, Bulgaria, the Ukraine and Serbia.

The development of Church Slavonic

By the end of the ninth century the monks had been forced out of Moravia and transferred their missionary activity to Bulgaria. This was also of significance for the story of Russian Orthodoxy, for the first written texts, lives of the saints and so on, were in the South Slavonic tongue—which is the basis for the Church Slavonic used in the liturgy of the Russian Orthodox Church today.

It has to be stressed that Russian Christians love the ancient language of prayer and worship. As a Westerner, visiting Orthodox friends, I used to plead for a modernized liturgy. But Russians do not want to update their worship. Church Slavonic language is holy, they say; it doesn't carry the coin of commerce. For an educated person, Old Church Slavonic poses few problems. Children of believing families learn the prayers from their earliest years. Prayer books are now produced with some explanation of the more archaic forms and children, who in any case love the sound of new words, have no difficulty with the prayers their parents teach them. The upper classes in pre-revolutionary Russia used French from earliest childhood and grew up bi- or trilingual. Nowadays, English has become the *lingua franca* of Europe and many young Russian parents teach their children English nursery rhymes, the English alphabet along with the Russian one. Pop songs, adverts, all the most debased forms of the mass media boom out day and night in English. And so believing people cling more firmly than ever to their sweet-sounding Old Slavonic. 'If we are bilingual in the secular world, why not be so in prayer and worship?' they say. So then someone like me used to argue, 'Yes, well, but what about young people out in the street who have never been taught the prayers and don't understand Church Slavonic?' But my Russian friends reply, 'It's not a problem. Anyone who knows Russian will understand this older language and in a Christian family children will grow up learning these prayers from their mothers and will absorb the truth, which matters more than meaning.'

And I realize once again that I cannot bring Western prejudices to Russia, and least of all to its church. And, yes, there are peculiarities. For example, the Old Slavonic word for 'life' now means 'stomach', so 'eternal life' in church language sounds the same as 'eternal stomach' in modern Russian! But no one laughs. That's the important thing. The Russian Church, reviled and persecuted for almost the whole of the twentieth century, holds such a precious place in the hearts of the people that no one makes fun of it any more. No one wants to change it. 'It's ours!' And this word in Russian implies total acceptance.

'Which way of worship should we choose?'

However, back in the tenth century the question was not, 'What language shall we use to pray to God?' but, 'To which deity shall we pray?' As separate tribes formed themselves into something approaching a nation-state, they found that the old pagan religions which had been linked to the structure of the tribe were becoming outmoded. The tribes had been centred around a theocracy of sorts in which priests who could read auguries would dictate to chieftains how they should act. By the ninth and tenth centuries, however, the princely court was emerging as a centre of authority, and the old conservative pagan ways hindered its progress. Christianity, moreover, gave strong support to the power of princes—'the powers that be are ordained by God'. Romans 13:1

has become proverbial. A thousand years ago, the text unequivocably sanctioned the Christian conquest of pagan lands.

But Christianity had its risks too. Change always has its opponents and there were still forces on the side of the old pagan order powerful enough to make a ruler think twice about making enemies of them. Then, too, the newly baptized prince laid himself open to being dominated by foreign missionaries who, however loyally they might serve their new convert, had retained strong links with their former ruler, making a country which had only just embraced Christianity feel at best a poor relation, at worst a vassal state; perhaps rather in the way former Eastern bloc countries feel vis-à-vis the capitalist neighbours whose market they seek to join.

By the end of the tenth century, Vladimir of Rus still had quite a wide choice when it came to religion. His grandmother, Olga, had been baptized as a Christian and this formidable woman, who put not a few people to death before her baptism in AD955 when she was more than sixty, is now known as a saint. The old chronicles call her 'Olga the Wise'. The story of her baptism is wholly delightful; she not only received all the blessings of Byzantine Christianity, she managed to outwit the Emperor himself:

> When she was enlightened, she rejoiced in spirit, and in body; and the Patriarch gave her instruction in the faith, and said, 'Blessed art thou among Russian women, because thou hast loved light and hast forsaken darkness: the Russian peoples will bless thee to the latest generation of thy descendants.' And he enjoined on her the church system, prayer, fasting, and almsgiving, with keeping chastity in body. She bowed her head and stood taking in his teaching as a sponge drinks up water: then doing obeisance to the Patriarch, she said, 'By thy prayers, my lord, I shall verily be preserved from the snares of the enemy.'
>
> … After the baptism the Emperor summoned her and said, 'I desire myself to wed thee.' She replied, 'How canst thou desire to wed me, when thou thyself didst christen me and call me "daughter": thou well knowest how that is not lawful to Christians.' And the Emperor said, 'O, Olga, thou hast outwitted me.'

Old Russian chronicles, quoted Norman Stone,
The Russian Chronicles, 1990

Olga is described as the 'morning star which precedes the sun', although her sons reneged on their mother's faith and turned their country back to paganism. Vladimir himself first tried to create a system in which a plethora of deities, acknowledged by the peoples he ruled, would be worshipped through his Kievan state.

There were, however, political pressures. The religious and cultural work of those missionary priests from Thessalonika who transferred from Moravia to Bulgaria made the Slavic tribes there the dominant force in the Bulgarian state. Towards the end of the tenth century, the strength and vitality of the Bulgarian Christian nation led the Emperor in Byzantium to seek allies from further afield, notably the Kingdom of Kievan Rus, thus forging a mutual and highly significant relationship. Political ties were cemented by family ones. In AD988 Vladimir captured an important Byzantine Crimean outpost, married the Emperor's sister, Anna, embraced Christianity in its Eastern Orthodox form, toppled the statue of the god of thunder, built a church dedicated to St Basil on its site and led his country in baptism. Old pictures show Vladimir watching his subjects meekly enter the waters of baptism.

'God dwells there among men...
We cannot forget that beauty'

According to the old chronicles, before Vladimir chose Christianity he sent ambassadors to seek out representatives of the four main religions, Judaism, Islam and Western and Eastern Christianity. From the seventh to the tenth centuries the ruling élite of the Khazar peoples, who occupied the forests and steppes of what is now Ukraine and Russia, were Jewish or had adopted Judaism. Richly woven rugs and fine vessels show the affluence of this people—and must have made their form of religion attractive to Vladimir. About the time that Vladimir was making his enquiries into their faith, although the Khazars were being displaced by his own Kievan Rus, the sizeable Jewish population in Vladimir's territories—numbering perhaps about eight thousand —would be reason enough for the ruler to look seriously in the direction of Judaism.

The chronicler says that the ambassadors brought back reports that this was a most just religion, but one in which money should not be put to usury, neither was pork to be eaten. Islam too, they informed the king, also forbade the eating of pork and the drinking of alcohol—a turn-off for Vladimir, who exclaimed, 'Drink is the joy of the Russians, we cannot exist without that pleasure'. Islam—and this undoubtedly interested Vladimir, permitted polygamy. Vladimir was 'insatiable in fornication… a lover of women, like Solomon'—but few monarchs have allowed the bonds of matrimony to deter them from following their own pleasures, so he turned his attention to Christendom and sent his ambassadors to Germany and Byzantium. The envoys brought back reports of a Pope who reigned supreme as a temporal as well as a spiritual ruler, which didn't suit Vladimir. They also added, 'We saw no beauty in their churches.' But the ambassadors who had been sent to Byzantium came back with glowing reports. They had seen the great church of St Sophia the Holy Wisdom in Constantinople and declared that they were at a loss for words. 'We knew not whether we were in heaven on earth. For on earth there is no such splendour or such beauty and we are at a loss how to describe it. We only know that God dwells there among men and their service surpasses the ceremonies of other nations. We cannot forget that beauty…'

And if that were not enough, an extra nudge was given: 'Your grandmother, Olga, who was the wisest of all people, also chose the Greek system…'

Russian church architecture embodies Christian teaching

So Vladimir chose Orthodoxy. And to this day everything about an Orthodox church points to heaven—not in terms of soaring Gothic arches and pointed spires, but in the painted domes outside, the layout inside, including the ordering of the icons; all is designed to take the eye, the heart and mind from the earth to the very throne of the Ancient of Days. Nor is the beauty of an Orthodox service merely visual. The singing of the choir, the ring-ing of bells, the sound of prayers, the smell of incense, all add to the aura of holiness and enable the unsighted to participate in worship too.

An Orthodox church seeks to show forth in every detail the great truth: God is with us (Matthew 1:23). The Orthodox will quote Stephen's words at his trial: 'The Most High does not dwell in houses made with human hands' (Acts 7:48) or Paul's words in Athens: 'The God who made the world and everything in it, he who is Lord of heaven and earth, does not live in shrines made by human hands' (Acts 17:24). And: 'For we are the temple of the living God' (2 Corinthians 6:16).

God lives in us through the saving work of Christ and the indwelling of the Holy Spirit.

But when the goodness and loving kindness of God our Saviour appeared, he saved us, not because of any works of righteousness that we had done, but according to his mercy, through the water of rebirth and renewal by the Holy Spirit. This Spirit he poured out on us richly through Jesus Christ our Saviour, so that, having been justified by his grace, we might become heirs according to the hope of eternal life.

(Titus 3:4–7)

Orthodoxy is quite at one with Western Christians in this. Architecturally this truth is expressed by the central dome. And since God's plan—which, says Paul in Ephesians, he has made known to us in Christ—is 'to gather up all things in him, things in heaven and things on earth' (Ephesians 1:10), the central dome adorns the meeting place of the people of God to show that in church, just as in the kingdom of God, all things in heaven and on earth are united under Christ as head. It also aims to show that in Christ we are 'filled with all the fullness of God' (Ephesians 3:19).

An Orthodox church may be crowned with many domes, but the central one always represents Christ. A large central dome surrounded by four smaller ones signifies Christ and the four Evangelists, one which is in the centre of twelve domes may indicate Christ and the twelve apostles, also the twelve months of the year and the twelve major festivals of the Church; a large dome flanked by an outlying bell tower symbolizes Christ and his

Mother and so on. I recently heard a guide on a city tour of St Petersburg say that the five domes symbolize Wisdom—Sophia—and her daughters, Faith, Hope and Love, with the fifth dome being ourselves, but this is a popularizing of the theology behind the design of the roof of an Orthodox church.

Within the church the great Royal Doors into the sanctuary, where no woman may ever enter, open to reveal the Courts of Holiness, where Christ reigns in all his splendour. For there is the blue of heaven and the risen, triumphant Lord depicted on the wall and ceiling of the sanctuary. Folk, wearied with standing, with the harsh conditions of life outside, with the stringent demands of fasting laid down by the church and obeyed, look up and see the risen Lord revealed in all the wonder of prayerful art—and know blessing which people who sit on padded pews may never experience.

Inside, as well as outside, the way in which the church is built is designed to focus on the way in which all creation is at one in the love of God. To Orthodox eyes Western churches centre either on the table, the upper room of the last supper (Mark 14:15), or are simply understood as meeting places where people gather to hear the Bible expounded, sing hymns and pray. An Orthodox church, however, which contains both table and meeting place, is ultimately inspired by the city of God depicted in the book of Revelation: 'After this I looked, and there in heaven a door stood open… and there in heaven stood a throne… And the one seated there looks like jasper and carnelian…' (Revelation 4:1–3). And so in every Orthodox church the Royal Doors open to reveal the throne, which symbolizes the triune God, Father, Son and Holy Spirit. The throne, therefore is the focus of worship. The importance of the holy scriptures, the Word of God, is symbolized by the central place of the heavy, jewel-encrusted Gospel Book and the saving work of the Lamb of God is shown in the eucharistic offerings.

All around the throne are the angels and saints, those servants of the Word and of the Lamb whose praise is without end (Revelation 5:11). But the picture is incomplete without the people who complete that holy gathering, 'no longer strangers and aliens, but… citizens with the saints and also members of the household of God, built upon the foundation of the apostles and prophets, with Christ Jesus himself as the cornerstone' (Ephesians 2:19–20).

Everything about an Orthodox church is designed to illustrate this community of faith: believers who on this earth are joined through faith with the eternal praise and worship of the kingdom of heaven, are no less part of the rich and complex design of the church.

Externals express what we feel within

The place in which prayer is made is very important in Orthodoxy. The church is often called 'the temple', and indeed, the temple of the Old Testament is the prototype of an Orthodox church, which is seen to fulfil that of which the temple prefigured: the worship of God 'in spirit and in truth' (John 4:24). So although several of my Jewish friends have told me that the sumptuousness of Orthodoxy puts them off, there are in fact common roots with Judaism. Once, after a solemn service in which two young men of no more than twenty made their vows as monks and were symbolically shorn, clothed in dark cassocks and given new names, I caught a glimpse of the main celebrant—priest or bishop, I didn't know. But to me he was none other than the High Priest himself, in crown and ephod and all the apparel we read of in the book of Leviticus.

The robes of the clergy, priests and bishops are symbolic too: at their simplest there is an outer vestment marked with a cross, the 'garment of salvation', while the white robe shows forth the new creation in Christ Jesus (2 Corinthians 5:17). The priest wears it now, as he celebrates the liturgy, but one day all believers will be robed in white (Revelation 7:9). In Russian churches all priests wear a large cross on a metal chain, and of course the making of the sign of the cross has the dual meaning that Christ died on the cross for our salvation, and that as Christians we take the cross as the foundation of our lives: 'If any want to become my followers, let them deny themselves and take up their cross and follow me' (Mark 8:34).

In Orthodoxy externals are important aids to expressing what we feel within and vestments are considered an essential part of worship—they symbolize the salvation which we already have in Christ and 'wedding garments' we shall wear at the coming of the kingdom of God when the glory of the Lord will be revealed to all people and all creation.

The Orthodox Church doesn't offer its people Bible teaching as we understand it, though some priests in recent years have been more open to the idea. But young people who attend classes on Orthodoxy will be given the Bible as background. Scripture will be used to explain the meaning of their worship, but also the things they see about them in church will be visual aids to remind them of the teaching of the Bible. There is, of course, a very major difference in approach and understanding, but it simply isn't true to assume that the Orthodox are biblically illiterate.

And as for the uneducated and the poor, the physical expressions of Orthodox worship open a pathway into prayer and communion which more highly literate churches fail to provide, however informal they try to be, however much they unpack and explain. All through its thousand years of history visitors to Orthodox Russia have noted how even young children seem at home in the church and conversant with its elaborate rituals. A girl of twelve told me, 'I wasn't baptized when I was a baby, but in 1988 it was the Thousand Years of Christianity in Russia and Mum and Granny took me to church. I love God. I thought then that God was like a good, kind grandfather and Jesus was a good, kind uncle. I like going to church. I light a candle and I feel that I'm part of one big family and that makes me feel happy.'

A 'drop-in' centre for God?

For me, personally, one of the most important things I feel that Orthodoxy offers people is 'the beauty of holiness'. Put at its simplest, it offers the chance to draw aside from the crush of life, light a candle in a place redolent of prayer, and be at peace in a setting far removed from the rush and hurry of the everyday, a peace without words which needs no explanation.

When my husband studied at an Anglican theological college there was a lot of talk about 'folk' religion, about people using churches simply to be 'hatched, matched and despatched'. There was concern that this was not part of the church's mission; it didn't win new converts for Christ; it was basically a waste of time. But I thought then, and I think it far more strongly now, that these are great moments of opportunity. I think we expect too much understanding. We explain too much, and allow little place for mystery, little place for grace. My mother used to sing a song: 'In Brittany the churches all day are open wide, And anyone who wishes to may pray and rest inside...' Perhaps that's hopelessly idealistic for today's inner city churches, or for country parishes where one priest has to look after six or seven churches. However, we run 'drop-in centres' for the homeless and for people who make regular use of the mental health services; where are the 'drop-in' centres for prayer, for God? And if we did open our churches and the people who came in were those with time on their hands, not the managers, doctors, senior people in the city, but the disadvantaged, the poor, people who do not wash as frequently as we might like, people who are unable to sustain 'normal' behaviour for long —then perhaps that is the fertile desert God gives our churches. Perhaps we shall learn the real meaning of the Beatitudes, which are sung so regularly in Russia: 'Blessed are the poor in spirit, for theirs is the kingdom of heaven...' (Matthew 5:3ff). I feel sure that if churches keep their doors open, at times of tragedy, of national crisis, people will know where to turn.

Remember those packed churches in Poland? They tumbled a mighty empire.

There is, in fact, a tremendous hunger now in the West to rediscover holy places. Places where tragic accidents happen are quickly turned into shrines, with flowers, candles, toys, photographs of the child struck down in a car accident, of the victim of violent crime. At the time of the James Bulger tragedy, I thought, 'Why don't churches open their doors and simply invite people in, not to do it *our* way, but just to draw aside, light a candle, perhaps, write a message, leave a flower, say a prayer if they want to—simply feel at home?' The huge public reaction to the terrible killings at Dunblane, and also the outpouring of grief at Princess Diana's funeral, showed us how desperately people need this focus. I feel that this must be the way forward for Western

Christians—let's stop trying to explain things; stop locking our holy places up; open them up, let people come in, and God will do the rest in his way, in his time.

We may—and do—disagree with the Orthodox on many issues, but the Lord says 'there is need of only one thing' (Luke 10:42). And we cannot deny that an Orthodox church exists for prayer. Its doors are open and prayer is offered day and night. The basis of all that we hear and see—and smell—in an Orthodox church is worship. It literally illustrates Psalm 84:

> *How lovely is your dwelling place,*
> *O Lord Almighty!*
> *My soul yearns, even faints,*
> *for the courts of the Lord;*
> *my heart and flesh cry out*
> *for the living God.*
> *Even the sparrow has found a home,*
> *and the swallow a nest for herself,*
> *where she may have her young—*
> *a place near your altar,*
> *O Lord Almighty, my King and my God.*
> *Blessed are those who dwell in your house;*
> *they are ever praising you.*

> *(Psalm 84:1–4, NIV)*

The lovely lyricism of that psalm is worked out in every Orthodox church, where structure, design and symbolism are all an open door to heaven. Even the bells which call people to worship are understood as a shepherd's pipe, the summoning of the Good Shepherd, who leads his flock to green pastures, where they may lie beside still waters, even in the valley of the shadow of death (Psalm 23).

People may not be taught, in the way we understand the term, but poor lost souls, the sparrows and swallows, the homeless, the young, who enter the open church have 'a place wherein to rest'.

CHAPTER 4

ICONS:
'WINDOWS TO ETERNITY'

PSALM 103:1

Bless the Lord, O my soul,
and all that is within me, bless his holy name.

Recently, I asked an American teacher who had studied in Moscow what he remembered about his visit to an Orthodox church. 'Icons,' he said. 'There were so many of them all over the church.'

I asked someone else what the word 'icon' conjured up for her and she said, 'Something like a very old, precious painting, something quite small. I would think, in religious terms, a picture of the Virgin Mary, for instance.'

'Have you ever seen an icon?' I wondered.

'I've seen postcards; I've never seen a real one... My impressions were that they seemed lifeless, almost depressing, certainly very sombre. When I go to an art gallery I get involved in the pictures. I can imagine I'm there, in the painting, but not with this. I get the feeling of something very distant which doesn't feel close to me at all. When I said "precious", I guess they could be very ornate, covered in jewels...'

A dictionary definition of 'icon' is 'a picture with a religious theme used in Eastern Christian churches as an aid to worship'.

Icons are 'visual aids' in the sense that many of them are, in fact, the Bible in pictures. There are, of course, icons of saints, of church festivals, but the primary source of the icons is the Bible. It's interesting to note that in Russia people never talk about 'painting' an icon; an icon painter 'writes' an icon—and icons can be 'read'. Moreover, they can be 'read' by an illiterate peasant woman as well as by a theological student. Just as the Church exists for the whole human family, so the icons, those silent studies of biblical people, biblical events, are open to everyone to 'read'. It has been said that icons bear witness to the open doors of the kingdom of God and of each believer's personal place within that kingdom.

Icons are not idols

You shall not make for yourself an idol... (Exodus 20:4)

It's important to emphasize that icons are not graven images. Exodus 20:3–5 is just as much part of Orthodox teaching as it is in the West. It's true that the Orthodox treat the icons in church and in the home with great reverence, setting candles before them, bowing low and, after prayer, kissing the icon. It must be stressed that they are not worshipping the icon, despite erroneous pronouncements by Western visitors to the contrary. A very early traveller to Russia, the explorer Richard Chancellor, who, in the brief reign of Edward VI, tried to find the north-east passage to India, reported from Moscow (where he was well received with his entourage): 'They have no graven images in their churches but all painted—to the intent they will not break the commandment: but to their painted images they use such idolatory that the like was never heard of in England' (quoted W.H. Frere, *Faith in Russia*, 1918).

Coming closer to our own time, there's a story about two New Testament scholars. They were sisters and were affectionately known as the Giblews—their joint surnames were Gibson and Lewis. They travelled through Greece, Palestine and Syria in search of manuscripts of the Bible, often visiting Orthodox monasteries in their quest. Once, as they were sitting down to breakfast in the monastery guest room, they found their butter had come wrapped in a fragment of parchment. Their trained eye saw that this was not just any old piece of skin. They scraped off the butter, and saw that the parchment had been written on! They spent the rest of the day in great excitement deciphering the old Syriac—and realized they had discovered a very early text of the Gospel of Mark!

Good Presbyterians, they made little attempt to enter or understand the world of Orthodoxy whose guests they were, but on one occasion Father Abbot invited them to kiss the cross. There was no way they could decline, but, resourceful as ever, they said firmly in impeccable Greek, 'We salute the Saviour of the world who died on the cross...'

But in fact their scruples were quite unfounded, for this is exactly what the Orthodox believe too. When people bow before an icon they are honouring the Lord, whose feet they kiss; they are showing the same respect towards the saint before whom they bow as they show each other when they give and receive a threefold kiss.

Icons show forth the unseen

Let's return to our dictionary definition. An icon is a picture on a religious theme, but it is not a religious painting in the way we understand the term, like one of the Great Masters we see in an art gallery. My friend was quite right when she felt she couldn't get involved in an icon in the same way as she could in an ordinary painting, even a religious one. The concept of an icon is not to awaken devotion as such. Far from encouraging sentiment, an icon eschews it. An icon silently shows forth the unseen.

Western Christians know of the importance of art in faith. Rembrandt's *Prodigal Son* kneeling, with one torn shoe, one foot bare, before his nearly blind father, whose hands embrace the ragged son so tenderly, has become for many—thanks to Henri Nouwen's devotional study, *The Return of the Prodigal Son*—a real vehicle for understanding Jesus' parable. But an icon is different from a religious picture and has to be differently understood. My friends have explained this difference to me more than once.

Until Peter the Great undertook his reforms to westernize and modernize Russia at the beginning of the eighteenth century, all art in Russia was religious. The first secular paintings are, in fact, portraits, showing the influence of the long tradition of icon painting. On one occasion, however, friends took me an exhibition of nineteenth-century Russian religious art. Although they depicted scenes normally shown on icons: the birth of the Saviour, Mary Magdalene, the apostles and so on, the paintings were clearly in a different style, showing the influence of French and Italian painters. 'We don't like this style,' my friend said. 'It's too sentimental.' And she explained that in the true tradition of icon painting, the artist—or school of artists—seeks not to evoke, but to invoke; the icon invites the viewer to look within, and emphasizes not the exterior, but the interior, the life of the soul.

'Think of the cross our priests wear compared with a Western crucifix,' my friend went on. 'On a Western cross we see the Lord in his agony but an Orthodox cross is completely flat; the figure isn't raised from the background. The concern is to show the spiritual truth of salvation, to lead our thoughts within—like the tradition of prayer of the heart.'

An icon is a vehicle for prayer

'All that is within me...' (Psalm 103:1), all my inmost being, is what is important in the concept of an icon. An icon seeks to embody not illusion but reality, not a moment in time, but an eternal truth. The icon painter aims to move from what is concrete, fleshly, finite, mortal, to what is spiritual, timeless, immortal. For all its richness the art of the icon, like the language of the desert, is minimalist. This is what gives the icon some of its apparent remoteness, severity and distance. In the words of St Basil the Great, 'The word of truth... in the economy of the Spirit... is so brief and concise... that little means much' (quoted in *The Meaning of Icons*, Leonid Ouspensky, Vladimir Lossky, 1952). The artist's aim is simplicity and depth, whose true content could only be accessible to the spiritual eye. An icon is made with prayer, it is about prayer and it transmits the state of prayer.

An icon is not intended to be a likeness. It is an attempt to portray not the here and now, but the eternal. The earliest Christian art of the catacombs was symbolic—a fish, a lamb, a shepherd, a chalice, bread, and so on, but it was also unashamedly instructive, depicting the scriptures and the teaching of the Church in such a way as to represent particular events, but also to show their meaning in the scheme of salvation. It was a vehicle for teaching the gospel—and it is this very ancient and early Christian tradition which the art of the icon inherits.

A non-churchy way of understanding icons is to think of the importance in the home of the family album. Weddings, christenings, first birthdays, first day at school, these events are recorded by the camera and framed. We carry photographs of our loved ones when we travel, or place them on our desks at work. So when an Orthodox believer enters a church she knows she is in the company of her family who have gone before—the Lord, his mother, the saints in heaven, whose eventful lives are portrayed on the icons; and in her home she places small icons on the wall.

The 'beautiful corner' where a lamp burned continually before the icons, used to be the most important place in a Russian peasant's home and anyone entering would salute the Lord and the saints before addressing the members of the family.

Orthodoxy is proud to claim icon-painting as its highest form of art. The work of painting an icon is a spiritual work, which can only be undertaken with prayer. An icon painter, of course, is an artist. There is training and discipline, and the painter must understand the use of colour and form. But skill is not enough. The technique of icon painting can never be separated from its spiritual meaning. The icon painter is concerned to access the means of grace, the grace of silence, the grace of mystery. 'We paint the lives of saints, but we're concerned with something more than biography, we preach the Gospel, but we use no words. Our work uses created things, wood and linen, chalk, organic materials, egg yolk, lapis lazuli, gold, linseed oil, resins, amber. We offer them back to the Creator. "All things come from thee and of thine own do we give Thee" ... But we look beyond this world to the timeless,' an icon painter once explained to me.

Windows to eternity

This is no exaggeration. Perhaps we have to think of the music of Bach, or the English spiritual classic, *The Cloud of Unknowing*. The anonymous writer says that prayer is to pierce the 'cloud of unknowing' between ourselves and the infinite mystery of the Trinity with 'a dart of longing love', That is exactly what an icon does. An icon doesn't try to attract attention to itself. It points beyond. Icons have been called 'windows into eternity'. A window is small and bounded, the sky beyond is immense. But without the window we would not see the sky.

The sky speaks of peace, of escape from the humdrum, everyday world with its pressures and strains, of travel and far places, of God. This is especially true of a blue sky, and indeed the ancient Arabs believed that the colour blue, the colour of the sky, calmed the blood. The hunger in the developed world for the things of the spirit—and advertisers study this hunger and harness it to their product—is so great that, as a survey in *The Scotsman* noted recently, people are buying blue carpets, not beige, blue curtains, blue wallpaper. I read about this in a KLM flight magazine—this airline which prides itself on its quiet efficiency has chosen to be known by the colour blue!

Windows are so important that in some places, at least, it is actually illegal to be without a window in your place of work. Such is our perceived need of a glimpse beyond that in some places of work whole walls, even interior ones, have been made to look like glass.

And so as well as inviting us to look within, an icon takes us out, beyond ourselves. But it never seeks to be a 'holy picture', a portrait, or an illustration. Its purpose is to show the mystery of the action of God which works like yeast in dough, like the mustard seed in the deepest heart of things (Matthew 13:31–33).

Lady Julian of Norwich, who lived in the same dark and tragic century as the anonymous author of *The Cloud of Unknowing*, wrote: 'God comes down to the lowest part of our need'. This is the truth which an icon embodies. It is the work of human hands, it is made of destructible materials, but it is spiritual and looks to the things of the spirit.

The meaning of the icon-screen

In an Orthodox church, icons are displayed in rows on the iconostasis, the screen which separates lay-people from the sanctuary. It symbolizes the division which exists between the heavenly world and our life on earth, but at the same time it unites those two worlds, for God in Christ has broken down the division which was caused by human sin. 'For he is our peace... and has broken down the dividing wall, that is, the hostility between us,' writes Paul in Ephesians, and he continues:

So then you are no longer strangers and aliens, but you are citizens with the saints and also members of the household of God, built upon the foundation of the apostles and prophets, with Christ Jesus himself as the cornerstone. In him the whole structure is joined together and grows into a holy temple in the Lord.

(Ephesians 2:14, 19–21)

Orthodoxy takes this teaching quite literally and the iconostasis is designed to teach the truth which scripture proclaims: it divides the people from the sanctuary (and this is particularly true of Russian churches) but it is opened up at significant points of the service. The iconostasis is entered by the Royal Doors—we have to think of Psalm 24, 'Lift up your heads, O gates! and be lifted up, O ancient doors! that the King of glory may come in' (v. 7).

So great is the Lord of Glory that no gates are sufficiently high to allow him to pass. They must expand, be lifted up. This thought lies behind much of the pomp and ceremony, the colour and gold of Orthodoxy, and the Royal Doors are symbolically opened and closed during the drama of the liturgy. The Royal Doors represent the gates of paradise, closed by sin but opened by Christ's sacrifice for sin. They represent the threshold of heaven, the union of love between God the creator and his creation, and all the paintings in a Russian church are carefully arranged in systematic order to show forth this great truth.

On either side of the Royal Doors, to the right and left, are icons of Christ in glory and of his mother—placed in this order to proclaim the first coming of Christ as Saviour, born of the Virgin Mary, and the second coming in glory at the end of the age as king and as judge.

The icon of the Lord's supper, the most important sacrament of the Christian Church, is given the central place above the Royal Doors. This is to witness the truth that we are graciously invited to the marriage supper of the Lamb. 'And the angel said to me, "Write this: Blessed are those who are invited to the marriage supper of the Lamb"' (Revelation 19:9). The icon also depicts the

65

words of the Lord Jesus Christ: 'You may eat and drink at my table in my kingdom' (Luke 22:30).

To the side of the Royal Doors is a smaller door which is used by the deacons as they go in and out at various points of the service. The icons around these doors depict the first New Testament deacons, and also angels who are the servants of God. There is always an icon of the saint or the festival to which the church has been dedicated. The upper row of the iconostasis is dedicated to Old Testament prophets, including Moses the Law-giver, David and Solomon, the great prophet Elijah. They hold open scrolls with prophecies of the incarnation of Christ and they represent the teaching of the Old Testament, prefiguring the Church which Christ founded; and so the row below the prophets depicts the gospel. An icon of the resurrection holds centre place and grouped around it are icons depicting the twelve major festivals of the Church's year, summing up the gospel message. Archangels, angels, apostles, saints, the Virgin make up the rest of the screen, leaning, like corn bowed by the wind, towards Christ, a harmonious movement which takes our eyes to the Lord seated in glory upon his throne. Their gestures are reverent, they draw the spectator into their solemn dance of love and worship.

The word 'iconostasis' means simply a stand for icons, but in Russian churches it has become extremely elaborate and, with time, it developed to such proportions that it completely cut laypeople off from the sanctuary, though some priests, one no less a spiritual leader than St John of Kronstadt at the beginning of the twentieth century, favour smaller screens. But whenever a believer enters church the iconostasis spreads out before her the whole hierarchy of heaven, the prophets, apostles and evangelists, saints and martyrs, John the Forerunner, forming a great *Te Deum* with the persons of the Trinity the focus of it all.

The iconostasis in fact embodies the *Te Deum*, that ancient canticle of praise which Archbishop Cranmer appointed 'to be said or sung... daily throughout the year':

The glorious company of the Apostles praise thee. The goodly Fellowship of the Prophets praise thee. The noble army of martyrs praise thee. The holy Church throughout all the world doth acknowledge thee;

the Father of an infinite Majesty; Thine honourable, true and only Son;
Also the Holy Ghost the Comforter…

Icons embody Bible events

Other icons are displayed throughout the church and the walls
and ceiling may also be covered with frescoes which depict Bible
events from the creation, the fall, the flood, right through to the
marriage supper of the Lamb and the Bride.

It's not appropriate to stare around the church while the liturgy
is being sung, but if you enter the church at other times and look
around you, your eye takes in the entire Bible story.

When the Bible was forbidden in Russia, icons were silent witnesses which showed forth the scriptures, the story of people of
faith. The most famous, and probably the most photographed,
church in St Petersburg is the Church of the Saviour on the Blood.
Built in the late 1880s on the site of the assassination of Tsar
Alexander II (hence 'on the blood'), this church, whose spectacu-
lar domes are modelled on the ancient church of St Basil's in the
Moscow Kremlin, has become a real landmark for visitors, almost
a symbol of St Petersburg. This is quite ironic since Peter the Great
intended the city he founded on boggy marshland to be a Western
city and the first buildings, the Peter and Paul fortress, the
Admiralty building have soaring spires in imitation of the West.
They are, however, in keeping with Russian tradition, covered in
gold. Peter would have been dismayed at the Byzantine splendour
of the Church of the Saviour on the Blood.

After the revolution in 1917, churches were vandalized and
closed, blown up or used as metro stations, museums, workshops. When I first visited Leningrad there were only fifteen
churches left functioning in a city of five million inhabitants which
once had a church on almost every street. I've been told that
Stalin intended to blow up the Church of the Saviour on the Blood
too; fuses were set, but war broke out and Stalin needed the dy-
namite elsewhere. The church survived the war, but it remained
under scaffolding for over thirty years. It has now been repainted
and the golden domes, the blue and green, catch the sun and
attract the cameras.

At one time I arrived in what was still Leningrad on a Sunday and I very much wanted to go to church. But I was put up in a hotel on the main Nevsky Prospekt and the three nearest churches were not in operation. The Kazan Cathedral had been turned into a museum of atheism. The other two were both closed. I later found out that one, the beautiful German Lutheran Petri-Kirche, had been turned into a swimming-pool, and its pastor perished in the Gulag. The other, St Catherine's Roman Catholic Church, was also derelict, although the Latin text outside said, 'My house shall be called a house of prayer...' (Matthew 21:12). Both these churches are set back from the main street, as the non-Orthodox were different and had to be discreet.

I wandered down the canal bank towards the Church of the Saviour on the Blood, encased in wooden scaffolding. My Sunday service that day consisted of a slow walk round that massive building, looking up at the frescoes, the Lord in glory, his birth and death... There was plenty to feed my thoughts, and I found I was not alone. Quite a few people were doing just what I was doing, looking up at frescoes and viewing the Bible in pictures, the Bible which was officially mocked and still virtually unobtainable in print.

A year later I visited a Christian family. The father had been in prison for his faith, and the children, aged five and seven, had received Christmas greetings from an English Sunday School. The English children had drawn pictures of Rudolf the red-nosed reindeer ('Who is this?' wondered the children's mother), Santa Claus and Christmas trees. The Russian children drew pictures, too, for their English friends. They had drawn Easter pictures: the women carrying spices to the tomb, the Easter angel, and the risen Lord. There were no illustrated children's Bibles in Russia at that time— no Christian literature for children at all, no Sunday School in Orthodox churches. But these two little girls had drawn biblical scenes from the icons they saw in church and I saw then how icons can be a doorway into faith.

'I saw him and I sought him,' wrote Lady Julian. We 'see' the Lord by faith in our hearts. And we seek him in prayer. An icon is above all a vehicle for prayer.

We 'read' an icon

An off-putting feature for Western Christians might be that the art of an icon is extremely stylized and is steeped in tradition. As well as being minimalist ('less is much'), it is deliberately impersonal. The painter seeks to deny himself in the same way that a nun renounces self-expression in her attire. In an icon every gesture, every colour has a meaning. Once this has been explained it helps us 'read' the icon. Green, for example, is the colour of the Holy Spirit. At the Feast of Pentecost (which is celebrated together with the Feast of the Holy Trinity) churches are decorated with branches of green leaves, speaking of the renewal of life after the long cold winter. Green is also the colour of youth. If an icon depicts a young person, he or she will usually have a band of green in a veil, on a tunic. However, on the icon of the Presentation of Christ in the Temple, Anna the octogenarian prophet who 'began to praise God and to speak about the child to all who were looking for the redemption of Jerusalem' (Luke 2:38) is shown dressed in a veil and robe of green. She was filled with the Holy Spirit and is clothed accordingly. Red is the colour of martyrdom; gold is the colour of kingship; brown is the colour of the earth.

Christ is shown wearing deep purple and blue, symbolizing his sacrificial death and heavenly glory. His fingers are usually shown in blessing, the forefinger and middle finger raised, the others bent.

The Virgin Mary usually wears a dark robe with gold stars in her veil. She is never portrayed alone, but always holding her child. In one typically Russian genre of painting, the Virgin of Lovingkindness, the child is shown pressed against the mother's cheek —the embrace is formal and we feel that it is graciously given by the Son to the mother, rather than the other way round. His fingers are always shown raised in blessing, while Mary's point towards her child. She is also depicted holding the child on her arm, rather like a throne, and showing him to the world. Unlike the earlier art of Byzantium, these great Russian icons profoundly depict the humanity of Christ and his mother and teach the essence of the prophecy by the old man, Simeon—he sang of peace and predicted a sword (Luke 2:35). The mother is shown to be grieving for the coming passion in a silence too deep for tears (the faces of Christian mothers in Soviet Russia, Baptist and Orthodox, were marked with that same deep, unspoken sorrow). It has been pointed out that even the greatest Western artists, Raphael, Leonardo, could not imbue their madonna and child with greater warmth. It is a peculiarly Russian achievement. Western art of the high Renaissance perhaps achieved paintings which were more human, but not more moving than the dignified, solemn embrace of the Russian Child and Mother of Tenderness or Lovingkindness.

Lovingkindness, says St Isaac of Syria, is when a person's heart burns with such compassion for all creation that his or her eyes fill with tears, and the least pain suffered by the smallest creature wrings the person to the soul. This is exactly the quality caught by what seems to me the most tender and moving of all the icons of the Mother of Tenderness: the Vladimir Mother of God, where the child is truly shown to be Emmanuel—God with us—and the mother both holds and yet gives away her son. The icon powerfully embodies the meaning of grace; here is the love which, as Paul describes in 1 Corinthians 13, is not proud, nor self-seeking, but bears, believes and endures all things.

Some icons are credited with wonder-working powers. This is often because the icon has been carried into a battle in which Russia was on the winning side. This happened to an icon known as the Kazan Mother of God, which depicts the Virgin Mary holding her child high on her arm, so that she is a pulpit from which the Word is 'heard'. The child wears gold and is shown full face to the world, his hand raised in blessing. The mother's face is a blend of tenderness, motherly love and sorrow. It is as though, while she showers her son with love, her eyes look within to the sorrows which are to come.

This icon is one of the most popular in Russia. Its spirituality finds a deep resonance with this long-suffering nation, and particularly with its women, and it is copied over and over again. But the original Kazan icon is credited with wonder-working powers and this is its story. Kazan is in the part of Russia which belonged to the Tartars conquered by Ivan the Terrible in 1552. To celebrate his victory Ivan had a special crown made, his 'Kazan hat'. It was made of gold, studded with turquoises, rubies and pearls, an edging of sable covered the rim and the top was crowned by a single topaz. He ordered a cathedral to be built and dedicated to the Virgin of the Intercession, later known as St Basil's after a prophetic figure, a 'holy fool' whom Ivan honoured so much that he had his great new church built over holy Basil's grave. The magnificent cathedral, which expressed traditional Russian wooden styles in metal and stone, was built in the form of the eight-pointed star of the Virgin, with eight chapels to commemorate victories over the Mongol tribes.

After Ivan the Terrible (who, before he plunged himself and his country into the darkness of paranoia, was a very religious man) had won the city of Kazan for Russia, a young girl had a succession of dreams in which the Virgin Mary appeared to her, showing her where a hitherto unknown icon lay buried in the earth. None of the church or court authorities would listen to the girl, but she and her mother followed the instructions she had received in her dream and found the icon, which is now known as the Kazan Mother of God of Lovingkindness. The icon was carried with the armies who liberated Moscow from the invading Poles in 1612. Two hundred years later it inspired the army in their campaigns against Napoleon, and the great battle of 1812, which Russia won. The vast structure of Kazan Cathedral in St Petersburg was built as a thank-offering for the victory and called after the icon, which was transferred there. Under Communism the cathedral was desecrated, but the icon survived. During the Second World War, when the German front line came virtually to the edge of Leningrad, Stalin allowed a degree of religious freedom. The Kazan Mother of God was carried in procession around the city by starving, beleaguered people—and there are many who say that the amazing endurance of the people in a cruel siege of three years is thanks to the protecting powers of the infant Christ in the arms of his mother.

During those years of bitter cold and starvation, people cooked cats and broke up their furniture and burned their books for firewood. But icons were not burnt. When one of my friends was a tiny baby her mother took an old family icon of the Saviour the

Ruler of All (*Pantocrator*) with her and her baby daughter as they were evacuated across Lake Ladoga, the only route in and out of the beseiged city, heavily mined and constantly bombarded. Three convoys of starving mothers and children left the city. Enemy action destroyed two; the one with my friend survived. Not unnaturally, the family attributed their survival to the Lord in heaven—and to his presence with them on the icon, which has pride of place in their home.

My friend never gave way to the doctrines of Communism. She refused to join the Young Communists' League and was discriminated against. Now in the new Russia of riches and misery, she works as a house mother in a grim home for children from problem families. She was in great distress when two of the boys in her class came under the influence of satanists. Now she reports with joy that they are reading Christian books, including an illustrated Bible, and praying for their friend in a Young Offenders' Institution. When people talk about Russia 'opening up' for the gospel, we shouldn't ignore the faith of Orthodox Christians like my friend.

There are, of course, many other icons of apostles, saints and martyrs. The Apostle Peter is shown with keys, Paul with a book. John the Baptist is shown in rough clothing, with unkempt hair. The saints are manifold: St Nicholas, the patron of Russia, is very popular; so is St George who in later versions is shown on horseback, thrusting his lance down the dragon's throat. In the earliest versions he is shown as the prototype of a Christian soldier, his sword held upright, and many other martyr saints are shown in this position. Two martyr princes, Boris and Gleb, sons of Vladimir, who were murdered soon after they had embraced Christianity, are always shown together. Their deaths were the result of family feuding rather than persecution of Christians but they are described by the early chroniclers as having died with great meekness and true faith. 'It is not for me to raise my hand against my brother. I do not resist,' said Boris, 'I do not refuse.' He prayed and lay on his couch awaiting his assassins. 'When they had pierced Boris,' continues the chronicler, 'the cursed ones wrapped him in a tent, put him on a cart and drove him away while he was still breathing... One of them pulled out a sword and plunged it into his heart. Thus the blessed Boris died, receiving from Christ our God a crown among the just.'

His 17-year-old brother Gleb, hearing of the death of his brother, lamented and turned to prayer. While he was still praying his murderers came upon him. Like St Magnus of Orkney in the twelfth century, Gleb was butchered by his kinsman's cook. 'Like a spotless lamb he was offered as a sacrifice to God,' notes the chronicler (quoted in Grierson, *Gates of Mystery: The Art of Holy Russia*).

Boris and Gleb are shown in armour, adorned with red, true princes of Christ. They died for love of God. Their refusal to resist force, their meekness and humility, even at the cost of their lives are virtues much admired by the long-suffering Russian people, whose hallmark is endurance rather than reform.

The icon of the Holy Trinity by Andrey Rublev

One the greatest of all the icons is the one by Andrey Rublev which depicts the three mysterious beings who came to Abraham at the oaks of Mamre, and hence is an icon of the Holy Trinity.

Every morning and every evening the Orthodox pray to the triune God, Father, Son and Holy Spirit:

O, Most Holy Trinity, have mercy on us. Lord, cleanse our sins. Master, pardon our faults. O, Holy One, visit us and heal our infirmities, for Thy Name's sake. Lord, have mercy, Lord, have mercy, Lord, have mercy. Glory be to the Father, and to the Son and to the Holy Spirit as it was in the beginning is now and shall be for ever, world without end, Amen.

Such is the devotion of people in Russia to the Holy Trinity that, from the days of Olga the Wise right up until our own time, people of prayer have been vouchsafed visions of the Trinity. It has been said that 'the love of Russian ascetics for the Holy Trinity drew the Trinity Himself to the land of Russia' ('The Holy Trinity in Russian Spirituality', Archbishop Pitirim of Volokalamsk, quoted *RCL* Vol 3, Nos 4–5, July–October 1975). From the fourteenth century onwards the festival of the Trinity was celebrated as an occasion of feast and love. One of the most attractive of all the Russian saints, Seraphim of Sarov, spoke of 'the breath of life, breathed upon the whole world jointly by all the Three Persons of the Most Holy Trinity holding the four corners of the world in their hands.'

Andrey Rublev's icon of the Trinity was painted in the early fifteenth century, by a man vowed to poverty, chastity and obedience and, after a time of terrible war and disaster, vowed also to silence. Most people are agreed that the fourteenth to sixteenth centuries were the high point of Russian icon-painting and that among the great work of that time, Andrey Rublev is unsurpassed. No other painters achieved quite the same rhythm which is the dance of stillness; quite the same luminosity of colour. Born of his life of prayer, his icons are lit from within. His life was the subject of a film which had a profound effect on a Russia still suffering the yoke of Communism: *Andrey Rublev*, by Tarkovsky. The great icon of the Trinity is full of the ineffable, of light and harmony, grace and dignity, communion and union. It was housed for years in the Tetryakov museum in Moscow. A friend of mine wrote this poem:

> *Atheists guard the angels:*
> *the Soviets treasure*
> *that trinity of beings*
> *Abraham addressed as 'Lord';*
> *amid primitive violence*
> *the man who painted them*
> *tried to live a pure life.*
> *Their tranquility contains*
> *excess; the people blow*
> *kisses at the plate glass.*
> *Guards, guarded and angels*
> *make another trinity.*

John Bate

Andrey Rublev is mentioned by a writer delightfully called Epiphany the Most Wise, whose book was written in 1418 (he dates it 6926, as if from the creation of the world). Brother Andrey is mentioned here in connection with his brother monk and fellow artist, Daniil:

It is necessary for us to remember, and very wonderful, how the desire of our holy father, the Abbot Nikon, was fulfilled, for there went out from him (i.e. his monastery) the two charitable and well-doing elders and painters Daniil and Andrey, who at all times preserved spiritual brotherhood and great love for one another. Having adorned the walls of this church with their icons they have left them for all to see as a memory of lives which are pleasing to God and full of blessing.

Rublev's icon is based on the account in Genesis 18:1–15:

The Lord appeared to Abraham by the oaks of Mamre, as he sat at the entrance of his tent in the heat of the day. He looked up and saw three men standing near him...' Abraham offered hospitality which the three accepted. 'They said to him, "Where is your wife Sarah?" And he said, "There in the tent." Then one said, "I will surely return to you in due season, and your wife Sarah shall have a son." ... Sarah laughed to herself... The Lord said to Abraham, "Why did Sarah laugh? ... Is anything too wonderful for the Lord?"'

Many icon painters depict Abraham's house, the oaks, the three angels, Abraham and Sarah serving their guests, the meal, servants... But Andrey Rublev, with the eye of genius, or of very great humility and love, stripped his icon of all but the three heavenly beings, the angels who represent the Holy Trinity. The three winged beings are seated around a table on which stands a small golden chalice containing a minimal suggestion of the slain calf, the choicest of Abraham's herd, which represents the sacrifice of the Saviour who went 'like a lamb that is led to the slaughter' (Isaiah 53:7).

If these angels represent the triune God, how are they placed? We might expect God the Father to be given the central place, but the angel in the middle and the angel on the right incline their heads towards the one seated on the left; and the line of their heads, their haloes, their shoulders and hands, as well the inclination of the tree which is seen behind the central angel, show us that the being on the left is the first person of the Trinity. He wears a robe of light blue beneath a transparent robe of brown—blue for heaven and brown for the earth. Our eye is constantly drawn towards him. The action in the icon is the action of stillness and it focuses on God.

Behind him, Abraham's tent has become a house whose roofs rise above the halo of the angel on the left. The house blends in with the yellow-gold background and symbolizes the New Jerusalem, the City of God (Revelation 21). Its position aids our understanding as to the nature of the first being of the three, while the tree sketched lightly but tellingly above the second angel is the tree of life, with its 'twelve kinds of fruit, producing its fruit each month; and the leaves of the tree are for the healing of the nations' (Revelation 22:2).

The angels are united by smooth, flowing movements. They are united, too, by the blue each wears, but in each it is differently portrayed. They are almost identical and yet each has his own individuality, reflecting the unique work of each person of the Trinity. Because we 'read' an icon, the figures here are grouped in the order of the Creed, from left to right: 'I believe in God the Father... and in Jesus Christ His only Son our Lord...' The central angel wears regal purple and an overgarment of blue. We have already seen that these are the colours worn by the risen, glorified Christ, but as further confirmation of his identity his right hand lies on the table. The first and middle fingers are extended in blessing—and point towards the chalice with the sacrifice, while behind him, as we have seen, stands the tree of life, reminding us that 'he himself bore our sins in his body on the cross' (1 Peter 2:24). The line from those two extended fingers takes our eye to the third being, the Holy Spirit, who wears blue beneath an overgarment of lightest green. 'I believe in the Holy Spirit...' is the third statement of the Creed. The green of his cloak indicates the work of the Spirit who renews all things and gives them life. His right hand leads our gaze across to the Father, so does the positioning of his feet, for the whole icon is constructed on circles, symbolizing the endless unity and perfection of the Godhead. In the seventh century, St John Climacus compared faith, hope and love to the circle of the sun, 'but all together they emanate one radiance and one luminosity'. This is what we witness in Andrey Rublev's icon.

The angels hold long, slim rods, reminding us of the 'measuring rods of gold' of which we read in Revelation (21:15), and hence of judgment, and reminding us too of the Good Shepherd, whose rod and whose staff 'comfort me' (Psalm 23:4). The hallmark of the icon is harmony, the generosity and courtesy of the angels is expressed in the humility of the Father, the reverence made towards him by the other two. They are seated around the table, symbol of the place of sacrifice, but also the place of the feast, the eternal feast in heaven of which Jesus speaks in his parables, in which the praise and compassion we see in the book of Revelation is joyously fulfilled: 'For the Lamb at the centre of the throne will be their shepherd, and he will guide them to springs of the water of life, and God will wipe away every tear from their eyes' (Revelation 7:17).

In front of the table is a small, rectangular opening, symbolizing the door into the kingdom which has been opened by the sacrifice of the Lamb. As for the space between the heavenly beings, this is for you and for me, for the invitation is 'to eat and drink at my table in my kingdom' (Luke 22:30).

Andrey Rublev's 'Trinity' is a whole rich symphony, inexhaustible in its content, which endlessly delights and constantly conveys new meanings, new music, yet in its essential simplicity, joy and courtesy it reminds me of George Herbert's 'Love bade me welcome', that lovely English Christian lyric, with its timeless simplicity, the laughter at its heart. As I contemplate posters and reproductions of the icon which has survived fully six centuries of turbulent history, including war and revolution, I find myself echoing Herbert's poem with new understanding:

> *You must sit down, says Love, and taste my meat:*
> *So I did sit and eat.*

> *George Herbert (1593–1632)*

Andrey Rublev's icon invites us to sup with love eternal and triune, and as we contemplate the heavenly beings we are drawn in to a feast of endless joy.

CHAPTER 5

Abbreviations Lose their Meaning so 'WRITE THE GESTURE OUT IN FULL'

ROMANS 12:1

I appeal to you therefore, brothers and sisters, by the mercies of God, to present your bodies as a living sacrifice, holy and acceptable to God, which is your spiritual worship.

Spirituality is about the life within, but it doesn't forget about our bodies. We have seen that Orthodox worship involves all the senses: sight—flickering candle-flames become a focus for prayer, as does the solemn, remote gaze of the saints on the icons; the sense of smell is involved in the wafting clouds of incense, and so is the sense of sound—we hear the sound of bells, the singing of the choir; much of the eucharistic liturgy is a chanted dialogue between clergy and choir, in which the congregation, too, have a voice. People participate with gesture and movement as well as joining in the Nicene Creed, the Lord's Prayer and the repeated chant, '*Gospodi, pomiluj*', 'Lord, have mercy...'

Richard Chancellor, the sixteenth-century English explorer to Russia, took a rather typically prejudiced view of Orthodox worship. He wrote: 'They have the olde and newe Testament, which are daily read among them: and yet their superstition is no lesse... And as for their prayers they have but little skill, but use to say '*Aspodi pomele*'—as much as to say, 'Lord, have mercy upon me' (*Faith in Russia*, W.H. Frere, 1918).

This minimal lay participation seems too little in the Western view of worship. Our tradition encourages us to 'join in'. But every visitor to a Russian Orthodox church—even those who come with very critical, negative feelings—notice the way in which people participate not with their voices alone, but with their whole attention. And how they unabashedly use their bodies to worship the Lord.

People bow deeply from the waist down, make the sign of the cross, kneel, and prostrate themselves. And stand absolutely still, with their hands at their sides. You can always pick out a foreigner; he shuffles, leans against a wall or icon stand, puts his hands in his pockets, takes them out again, looks around, sighs, shuffles again... And gets told off by an elderly lady, who explains that we do not put our hands in our pockets when we pray!

All of this is sheer bad manners, at the very least, and not how the Orthodox understand devotion. The Orthodox stand with hands at the sides, they bow from the waist and make the sign of the cross repeatedly and profoundly, never sketchily.

If any want to become my followers, let them deny themselves and take up their cross daily and follow me. (Luke 9:23)

The Orthodox express this all-important command of the Lord in a physical way by making the sign of the cross. However, the way this is done is symbolic and full of meaning: you tuck the little finger and ring finger of your right hand into your palm, and bend the middle finger and first finger forward to touch the thumb. The pattern thus made reminds us of who God is: the thumb and two fingers touching stand for the Holy Trinity, one God and three persons, the folded fingers tell us of the dual nature of Christ—he is God and Man. The priests make the blessing raising two fingers and tucking the thumb inwards to join the folded ring finger and little finger, so here the teaching is the same, but now the raised fingers represent the dual nature of Christ and the folded three stand for the Trinity.

'God loves everything in threes' is an old Russian folk proverb. Prayers are often repeated three times, the sign of the cross is made many times, but often it is a threefold signing, in which the fingers of the right hand touch the forehead to show God is in my mind, the body, just below the waist, to show that God is in my life, and then the right shoulder and the left shoulder. A friend told me once that this represents the wings of the guardian angel overshadowing me.

A church without seats

Our behaviour is reflected by our furniture. A formal dinner around a candlelit table requires different behaviour than a buffet meal taken standing, or fish and chips which we eat perched on a bench by the sea... And one of the things which makes behaviour in a Russian Orthodox church very different from worship in other churches is that there are no pews. There's far greater freedom to move around, to come and go, but, perhaps paradoxically, within the flexibility, there's a greater sense of neighbourliness, of everyone standing together. It is totally unthinkable to put seats in an Orthodox church, though a bench is placed on one side where the weakest literally 'go to the wall', as they used to do in medieval cathedrals, to sit and rest. I have, however, seen very elderly people bring little folding stools to church to sit through the long Easter vigil. But since this is the 'Festival of all Festivals, the Feast of Feasts' which all the church year leads up to and centres around, and people pack the churches hours before the vigil begins, there's a very real danger that anyone sitting on a little low stool would be knocked over in the crush.

Standing together—a physical expression of unity

One of the stated aims of standing together to participate in the liturgy is to express our unity in Christ as one body. 'And let us consider how to provoke one another to love and good deeds, not neglecting to meet together, as is the habit of some, but encouraging one another...' I have seen Hebrews 10:24 explained in this way: believers shouldn't enter church on Sundays to pray private prayers in the side aisle, as they may do at other times when no formal service is in progress, but 'not neglecting to meet together' everyone should stand together and participate in the liturgy as one. The Orthodox understanding of lay participation is that we enrich the body as a whole by our presence together. People may come and go during the long service and move about the church buying candles which they place before some particular icon, but the focus is on the progress of the eucharist, which everyone stands together to celebrate.

This sense of unity is very important. Prayer is spiritual warfare and if a believer prays alone, the teaching runs, he does not pray at all. We bring our own God-given personality into worship—but it is the joining of each individual with the prayer of all the church which brings spiritual strength.

'When we meet together in church we pray together as one body in unity of mind, heart and spirit' is the received teaching of the Orthodox. If the long church services seem wearisome, it is a sign that people are not truly joined together in spiritual unity. The idea of coming to church is to be together, and the sense of community we find together is an expression of our real union in the Holy Trinity. The divine liturgy is not for the person who wants to pray only in the quietness of the heart; that can be done before or after the service; it can be done at home. The services of the church are for all the people of God who pray together with one another, with Christ and with God.

So people stand together to pray. They stand as a sign that they rejoice that Christ is risen. The word for 'Sunday' in Russian is the same as the word for 'resurrection'. People may kneel during weekday services, but on Sundays, except during Lent, the custom is to stand.

Standing together—an act of obedience to Christ

It is also stressed that the Lord Jesus told us to stand when we pray. 'Whenever you stand praying...' he says in Mark 11:25.

Standing together—an acknowledgment of angels

'It is especially undignified to pray sitting,' Tertullian wrote in the second century, 'for the angel hosts stand before the Throne of God in fear and awe. It looks as if we're praying unwillingly, irreverently. We look as if we're tired.'

The Bible certainly tells us that the angels in heaven stand in the presence of God. In Luke's Gospel we read, 'Then there appeared to him an angel of the Lord, standing at the right side of the altar of incense... "I am Gabriel. I stand in the presence of God"' (Luke 1:11, 19).

And the great assembly in heaven, who worship the Lamb before the throne, do so standing, as do the angels:

After this I looked, and there was a great multitude that no one could count, from every nation, from all tribes and peoples and languages, standing before the throne and before the Lamb, robed in white, with palm branches in their hands... And all the angels stood around the throne and around the elders...

(Revelation 7:9, 11)

These verses are all quoted to underline the importance of standing to pray. I find it tedious, tiring, not least in winter when I'm weighted down with a heavy coat and boots. I often long for a respite, for a bench however low, for a chance to sit. But no, people stand. It is in fact unthinkable for the Orthodox to pray in any other way.

The significance of gesture

One very important thing I have taken away from my time in Russia is the significance of gesture, not just shaking hands and kissing when friends meet and part, though that's important too, but the spiritual benefit of the act of expressing our prayer with the movement of our bodies. Paul says, 'I appeal you therefore, brothers and sisters, by the mercies of God, to present your bodies as a living sacrifice, holy and acceptable to God, which is your spiritual worship' (Romans 12:1).

When the charismatic renewal was sweeping through our churches in the 1970s, many found it embarrassing and difficult to raise our hands in praise. And yet we discovered a great release and freedom when we did so.

Look at almost any manual on prayer and you will read suggestions about the way we may use our bodies: we may practise silence and stillness in order to 'centre down' as we come to pray; we may extend our hands with their palms down, letting go, releasing hurts, before we lift them to the Lord, ready to receive from him, to praise him; we may kneel, sometimes with the help of a prayer stool, lie on the floor, sit on a firm, straight-backed chair, establish a prayer place in our own homes, light a candle, focus on a cross, a picture, a word of scripture... and so on.

But that's in small groups or when we're alone in our own homes. In churches our public worship tends to be rather static. We sit or stand in rows and do not move much from our seats for fear of creating a disturbance, making a noise. We are heavily dependent on books, often being required to use three or four different ones in the course of a service. We may clap our hands, or raise them; we may even laugh and chat and embrace as we offer the Peace, but generally our movement in worship is restricted. We're very aware of our neighbours and we're shy of expressing devotion to God.

The importance of knowing the right way to behave came home to me in Poland. When Karol Wojtyla was made Pope, the ceremony was shown on Polish television. So what? we may think. But this was in 1978 and even in Poland—where the Catholic Church, from the previous Cardinal (who was imprisoned for three dark years) to the humblest peasant, had won a far greater freedom than anywhere else in Eastern Europe—religious life was still severely circumscribed. There were Catholic publishers and Catholic shops, but it was all tucked away and hidden. For example, once, on a train journey, I pulled out a novel by a well-known Catholic writer—and the fact was commented on by my fellow passengers. No Christian voice was heard in the media in those bleak years. So it was truly amazing that this service, from a non-Warsaw Pact country as well, was being shown in entirety on State television.

And everyone gathered around to watch. If you didn't have a television yourself, you went round to the neighbours. It was like Merseyside when Liverpool are playing a Cup Final. Not a soul in the streets. One man, a card-carrying party member who hadn't been to church for years, who actively worked for the avowedly non-Christian State, sat with his wife and daughter, riveted to the television screen. Like most people, he wept. And at the solemn moment, when the words were spoken, 'This is my Body...' and the Host was raised, he found himself on his knees in front of the television set—and discovered, with tears streaming down his face, that his wife and daughter were kneeling beside him. His life was changed at that point. He tore up his party card and turned back to God.

Using our body helps us
express our commitment to Christ

This man's body had found the way ahead of his conscious thinking. The gesture he made determined his subsequent decisions. Evangelists often invite people to 'come forward' to indicate that they have chosen to follow Christ. Here the physical action underlines what the heart has already decided. In the incident I'm relating, this man found that his body worked first. But in his earliest childhood he would have been instructed at home how to behave in church, he would have gone to Mass and received communion, and so he not only knew the significance of what he watched, he knew how to respond.

Children too small for words may learn the act of prayer

By and large, in the West, kneeling has gone out with kissing hands, bowing and curtseying. At home we may teach little children to fold their hands and close their eyes (how hard that is for a child), but a mother daren't close her eyes for long and we adults seldom fold our hands. Perhaps we hold hands round the table before a meal. Yet to stand and make the sign of the cross at the start of a new day, before a meal, before bed, engages the whole family. A friend of mine always signs herself with the cross as she leaves the house and says, 'Lord, save me and protect me.' She never allows her two sons to leave the home without blessing them, and they have got into the habit too, and as they unlock the door, ready to dash out on their affairs, they make this gesture of trust and hope in the Lord.

Friends similarly bless one another as they say goodbye, a gentle courtesy. Perhaps it's something we can put into practice too in our family life. We may be too rushed to spend long in family prayers, but if a parent is around to see children off to school, once they've sorted their schoolbags, checked they've got their homework or packed lunches, a quick word of blessing, accompanied by the sign of the cross, is like a kind of holy kiss which the child takes on his or her way.

And as far as tiny children go, I have seen that in Russia children too small for words learn the act of prayer.

'Don't laugh in church!'

The downside of this is the critical attitude in Russian churches, the sharp reprimands that children—and adults—receive if they act without due solemnity in church. At a baptism recently, at the end of the service, the aunt of the little baby who was being baptized exchanged smiles and whispered comments with me, amused at the behaviour of the toddlers and babies who had been baptized—and not just dipped in water, but anointed with oil and then myrrh, had a token lock of hair shaved from their heads, and much, much more. Morning prayer had long since finished; the baptisms had taken place; we were getting ready to leave, but even so an elderly woman came across to us and said reprovingly, 'Don't laugh in church!'

And I recalled an incident another friend had shared. The service was over; the Royal Doors were shut; the main lights had been put out; only a few candles still burned on their stands. Nearly everyone had gone home, and my friend and someone else she knew were buying candles and cards from the kiosk at the back of church. They chatted and laughed—and were told off by the woman who was selling the things in the kiosk. 'We do not laugh in church. It doesn't say anywhere in scripture that the Lord ever laughed.'

My friend was so stunned she went straight home and checked. And, true enough, we read that Jesus wept (Luke 19:41; John 11:35), but not that he laughed!

But it's hard to believe that the Lord, who attracted crowds of simple folk, to whom children ran to be blessed, was sad and severe. Surely when Jesus went to eat with Matthew and his friends, with Zacchaeus, he laughed. When we think of the brilliant story-teller who gripped great crowds with his parables, the healer who took the twelve-year-old girl by the hands, called her back to life from the sleep of death and organized her breakfast, the teacher whom the fishermen left their livelihood to follow, who called vacillating Simon Peter the 'Rock', John and James the 'sons of thunder'... can we really think that Jesus never laughed?

They think so in Russia. The Bible is written in archaic language; the icons never show Christ with a smile, and some make him seem very severe... 'No,' all my Russian friends have said, Orthodox and non-Orthodox, 'I never have the impression that Jesus ever laughed.'

Agape life, real community, is not seen in today's Russian Orthodox Church

Orthodox friends who have visited Scotland tell me they treasure the way people are relaxed in church, the way there is a genuine sense of love, the way people give way to one another as they reverently move forward to receive communion.

'Whereas here,' one of my friends said, 'people behave exactly as they do in any other public place. They push and shove, even when they're going forward to receive communion. The priest has actually said, more than once, 'Don't rush and push, there is plenty for everyone!'

We agreed that part of the problem is that there are still far too few churches, especially out in the housing blocks. All the same my friend concluded wistfully, 'I wish our people could learn from yours how to behave in church!'

And this is true. In spite of the teaching that our standing together expresses our unity as the body of Christ, there is no real sense of *agape* life in Russian Orthodox churches today. This is partly, as we've seen, because Communism wiped out church life. Believers who met together in their homes, Baptist or Orthodox were dragged off to the KGB, imprisoned and treated with the harshest severity. The young people who formed the Christian Seminar in Moscow in the 1970s did so because they discovered that the Church had little place for them. 'New problems awaited us within the sacred portals of the Church,' wrote Alexander Ogorodnikov. 'On the one hand, our involvement in the Church was hindered by a pagan element of intellectual pride, on the other by a lack of flourishing religious community life within the Russian Orthodox Church which deprived us of the opportunity to serve the Church actively' (*RCL*, Vol 7, No 1, 1979).

It is good… to write the gesture out in full,
the whole beautiful and weighty word: reverence.

In Russian churches I may long for a simpler service, a greater freedom of what we call fellowship, but away from Russia I long for more reverence, more beauty in our worship. Because Orthodoxy is so much about using your body I have come to feel ham-fisted without the use of appropriate gestures in prayer.

In a collection of stories which he wrote after visiting Russia and meeting Tolstoy, the Austrian poet Rainer Maria Rilke recounts a dialogue about Russia between himself and a neighbour, a man too lame to walk or stand.

'… All the ceremony, for instance. You speak to the Tsar as you would to God.'

'Oh, so you don't say, "Your Majesty"?'

'No, you call them both "Little Father".'

'And you kneel to them both as well?'

'You throw yourself down before both of them, touch the earth with your forehead, and weep and say, "I am a sinner, forgive me, Little Father." We Germans, seeing that, call it unworthy slavery. I think differently about it. What does kneeling signify? It is meant to express reverence. But you can do that well enough by uncovering your head, a German would say. Well, yes—raising your hat, bowing—they are also in a way expressions of it, abbreviations that have come about in those countries where there was not so much room that everybody could throw themselves on the ground. But abbreviations we soon use mechanically, no longer aware of their meaning. That is why it is good, where there is still room and time to do so, to write the gesture out in full, the whole beautiful and weighty word: reverence.'

'Yes, if I could, I too would kneel down,' mused the lame man.

Stories of God, *Rainer Maria Rilke, 1912*

'To write the gesture out in full…' That is what I have brought home from Russia: the importance of being unhurried, of acknowledging illness, for example, and giving time to my body to recover, not popping antibiotics. My Russian women friends know which kinds of food, cooked in which way, are good—or bad—for various ailments. People have a holistic approach to therapy—not surprisingly when medicine is appallingly conspicuous by its lack of care. They use massage, herbs, berries, daily doses of raw garlic to keep themselves well. Instant food has appeared in the super-markets, but its price is way beyond what my friends can afford. They do not have food processors, either, or electric kettles. Tea is drunk around a table with cups, saucers, sugar and something sweet, preserves or honey, not with mug in hand propped against a kitchen worktop, or sitting watching television, or at a desk. There is no way in which a Russian family would try to 'abbreviate' cuisine, far less religion. For another way in which the Orthodox use their bodies (and here lay-people, and especially women, have an important—if traditional—part to play) is that the Church still keeps the fast as well as the feast.

Keeping fast as well as festival

The Church is a wise mother, say the Orthodox, who not only gives us spiritual food but teaches us to deny our bodies in order to learn that 'the joy of the Lord is our strength' (Nehemiah 8:10). Like Judaism, the influence of Orthodox faith is in the kitchen as well as in the formal assembly. Women are relearning how to make that melt-in-your-mouth Easter delicacy, the white cheesecake called *Pascha*, and the rich *kulich*, full of eggs (and eggs and dairy products have been forbidden for six long weeks.) On Holy Saturday, that lull between the solemn sorrow of Good Friday and the radiant joy of Easter, mothers and children bring their Easter fare to church for the priest to bless. Once again this is an aid to teaching the faith to the very young. Children who can't under-stand long prayers and sermons remember the warmth of the church, sombre in its mourning in memory of the death of Christ, but already full of the hope of the resurrection.

They may come while the morning liturgy is being sung, and over and over again the voices of the choir will sound through the quiet church: 'When you went down into death, O Deathless Life, you destroyed death with the light of God: when you raised the dead from the pit, the Heavenly Powers cried, "O Lifegiver, O Christ our God, glory to you!"' (1 Peter 3:18–19 says: 'He was put to death in the flesh, but made alive in the spirit, in which also he went and made a proclamation to the spirits in prison.')

The anthem continues: 'The Angel appeared to the myrrh-bearing women at the tomb and cried, "Fragrant myrrh serves the dead, but Christ is alien to corruption."' (Mark 16:1, 5; 1 Corinthians 15:42–45).

I have noted in my own prayer book the following words for the Eve of Easter from Eastern Orthodox liturgies: 'Today a grave holds him who holds all creation in the palm of his hand. A stone covers him who covers the heavens with glory. Life is asleep. Hell trembles and Adam is freed from his chains' (1 Corinthians 15:20–22).

Children participate in the preparations for the festival, helping their mother paint the boiled eggs which people will break at Easter, tapping each other's eggs together with the joyful words, 'Christ is risen', 'He is risen indeed!'

One has to say, this is very much what mothers do with their children—Russian fathers leave domestic chores to their overworked wives.

In the West, too, the Church traditionally kept both fast and festival. But commercialism has taken over the festival and squeezed out the fast. Putting both back is crucial in our 'shop till you drop' society—and paradoxically the best way to make the festival shine is to celebrate the fast.

Fast food in Advent

One way of opting out of the 'run-up to Christmas' is to keep Advent—not just by lighting candles, but also by having fun together with your family, with your friends as you experiment in the kitchen and explore the meaning of 'fast food'—in other words, a meal based on fruit, cereals and vegetables, rather than on meat, fats, dairy products and so on. The Christmas dinner tastes all the better if you've been a bit abstemious beforehand! As it is, most people have been eating turkey dinners and mince pies since the first of December and are fed up with feasting long before Christmas Day. Here is another serious abbreviation. We've cut

Advent almost out of existence. I should like to reclaim holy and solemn season of Advent, read the great prophecies of Isaiah, the Advent prayers—we can add a new one each week as we light the four candles, one by one:

O, Wisdom who comes from the Mouth of the Most High, you fill the universe and hold all things together in a strong yet gentle manner: come and teach us the way of truth.

O Adonai and Leader of Israel, who appeared to Moses in a burning bush and gave him the law on Sinai, O come and save us with your mighty power.

O key of David and sceptre of Israel, what you open no one can close, what you close no one can open, O come to lead the captives from prison and free those who sit in darkness and the shadow of death.

O King whom all the peoples desire, you are the cornerstone which makes all one. O come and save us whom you made from clay...

If we concentrate on Advent we won't need to light the Christmas tree lights until Christmas Eve, when we say: 'O rising Sun, you are the splendour of eternal light and the Sun of justice, O come and enlighten us, whom you made from clay...'

On Christmas Eve (which is still 6 January in Russia) the Orthodox sing: 'While all things were in silence and night was in the midst of her swift course, thine Almighty word, O Lord, leaped from Thy royal throne...'

When we stop abbreviating Advent, we keep Christmas in full

And then, having kept Advent with as little tinsel as possible—and preferably none—I should like to reclaim the Twelve Days of Christmas when we can stuff ourselves full, visit our friends, party and carnival the midwinter gloom away. For when we stop abbreviating Advent we keep Christmas in full until we reach the mysterious and majestic Feast of Epiphany, when:

The Wise Man finds weeping in the crib him whom he sought for shining in the stars... and ponders in profound amazement over what he sees there: heaven on earth, earth in heaven, man in God, God in man and him whom the whole universe cannot contain confined in a tiny body. And immediately on seeing, he professes with mystical gifts that he believes and does not argue: he acknowledges God with frankincense, the King with gold, with myrrh the mortal one destined to die.

Peter Chrysologus, quoted in From the Fathers to the Churches,
edt. Brother Kenneth CGA, 1983

At the major seasons of the Church's year and particularly at Christmas, with its glut of candlelit carol services and nativity plays, it's a relief to turn to the austere, stately words of the Orthodox tradition: 'What shall we offer thee, O Christ, who for our sakes hath appeared on earth as man? Every creature made by thee offers thanks. The angels offer a hymn; the heavens, a star; the magi, gifts; the shepherds, their wonder; the earth, a cave; the wilderness, a manger. O God from everlasting, have mercy on us.'

'Post early for Christmas...' Did four short words ever so mislead? Let's get away from the great rush of gift-grabbing. All right, we'll be in a minority, but so what? Mary and Joseph were in the minority, too, when they were shut out from the warmth of the inn, the place of feasting and hospitality.

The King, before whom the angels of fire and spirit tremble, lies in the bosom of a girl and she cradles him in a manger. The heaven is the throne of his glory, yet he sits on Mary's knee. The earth is his footstool yet, a baby he crawls beside her. He measures the stars. Before him earth is dust, yet on that dust he walks, and has no home.

Adapted from St Ephraim the Syrian

Sanctification is a state, but it is also a process...

Our Christian life is a pilgrimage. Paul reminds us that we have 'taken off (our) old self with its practices and have put on the new self, which is being renewed in knowledge in the image of its Creator' (Colossians 3:9, 10, NIV).

Sanctification is a state, but it is also a process, and the ancient fasts and feasts of the Church, Western and Eastern, which are still kept by the Orthodox help us to renew the new Christ-self as we follow in our prayer life the path which was trodden by the Lord.

Into the wilderness

And so the nativity leads us into the adult life of Christ which, after his baptism, takes him—and us—into the wilderness. The season of Lent (which is an Old English word for 'spring'—and still is in Dutch!) has been abbreviated so completely it has come to mean little more than a well-meaning attempt at 'giving up' things we like and putting money into boxes for charity. All well and good, but it is still an abbreviation.

In Russia the season of the fast once again takes the faith into the kitchen. And once again I get cross, for I think that this strict fast is all right for monks in monasteries in Greece or Georgia, where there are plenty of tomatoes, of vegetables, even fruit, but in poor snow-bound Russia, where a cucumber is a luxury in the middle of February...?

But no: people fast. The Church prepares them for it for five weeks beforehand with carefully prepared services which focus around the meaning of penitence—each Gospel reading on the Sundays before the Great Fast actually begins is centred around fundamental aspects of repentance.

So the Church reads the story of Zacchaeus, the sinner who desired Jesus so much that he went to great lengths to see him. And the Saviour honoured his search—and did far more than Zacchaeus asked for (Luke 19:1–10). So we must ask ourselves, how much do we desire to meet Christ?

The next week focuses on the majesty of humility—the story of the pharisee and the tax collector, which reminds us of the sin of religious pride. The tax collector's prayer, 'God, be merciful to me, a sinner' (Luke 18:13), sets the tone for the coming season of penitence.

There is one more Sunday before clergy and believers are asked to respond to the solemn, yet joyful gospel message by fasting and to prepare the way the joy of repentance is summed up in the reading for the day: the parable of the Prodigal Son (Luke 15:11–31). The prayer is: 'I have wasted with sinners the riches Thou gavest. Now I utter the prodigal's cry unto Thee, O bountiful Father...'

The lost son had to make a decision to return home where he found the joy of forgiveness and the Great Fast helps us to recognize that we are exiles from our heavenly home, that our vocation is to return to our Father (v. 22).

The next Sunday, meat is omitted from the diet and the Gospel reading is Christ's great parable on compassion, with its royal welcome coupled with solemn warnings of the last judgment (Matthew 25:31–46). And here too the inner meaning of all our spiritual effort is shown. It is love—and not just a coin in a can for Christian Aid, but active involvement with the 'least of these' whom the Lord may put in our path today.

Russian Orthodoxy is accused of neglecting social concern. Russia itself suffered for eighty years from a philosophy in which social activists sacrificed the personal for an end which claimed to work for the common good. But the Lenten readings teach that Christ wants us to look beyond the labels with which we classify the needy and see our brother, our sister in the hungry, the sick, the prisoner, the poor.

Carnival before the austerity of the Fast

And so comes 'Forgiveness Sunday'. It's known as 'Cheese-fare Sunday' as the fast now begins in earnest. But the whole week before is a great time of pancake eating. It's the carnival of *Maslenitsa* —the equivalent of our Shrove Tuesday, only Russians eat pancakes all week.

Maslenitsa, which derives from the word for butter or oil—*maslo*—used to be a time of great festivity before the revolution. You ate dozens and dozens of pancakes (the little pancake is round, like the sun, and the festival has its origins in pagan rites of spring). The purpose was to use up butter, eggs, milk—the fare which would soon be taken out of the diet by Lenten austerities.

Maslenitsa, from all accounts, was a time for fun. People rode in sledges over the ice-bound rivers. The Tsars built huge palaces of ice. There were masked balls when the Tsar might dance with a shopgirl. Music played, whole choirs stood out on the ice and sang in open-air concerts in sub-zero temperatures. There would be impromptu outbursts of singing—for the Russians are a people of song—and vodka was of course downed in great quantity and variety! Roundabouts and swings and fairs of all kinds added to the joviality until the eve of Cheese-fare Sunday. Then everything shut down. The music was silenced. The shows were cleared away. No more ballets, operas, plays, the only concerts allowed would be of religious music. From the Tsar downwards, everyone observed Lent; and in church the clergy still lay aside their bright vestments and wear solemn black, while priest and people prostrate themselves and ask one another for forgiveness, bowing down to the ground.

When my husband and I used to visit Russia secretly, one of the books it absolutely wasn't possible to bring in, but which all our friends asked for, was called *Great Lent* by Fr Alexander Schmeman. This gentle book, which was branded by Soviet Customs as entirely unsuitable for its citizens, has been earmarked by the new regime for burning. Recently Fr Schmeman's books, together with writings of other émigré priests, were publicly burnt in Yekaterinburg at the command of the local bishop, an ominous sign from an out-of-touch, repressive hierarchy. *Great Lent* stresses that the time of the fast is a time of holy joy. The Great Fast is a time of 'bright sadness' when we 'put on' the love and joy of which Paul writes in Colossians 3. We recall the words of Jesus, 'Whenever you fast, do not look dismal' (Matthew 6:16), and this is the crux of the Great Fast. It is not a time for being gloomy, for Jesus himself showed the way and overcame temptation by his faith in the Word of God. The Fast is a time when we express our love for God and for others—and feel that love grow as we learn the deep sense of the words in John's Epistle: 'This is the victory that conquers the world, our faith' (1 John 5:4).

'This pleasant time of blessing'

It is a time for forgiving others, a time to learn of God's mercy and the choir sings:

Let us begin the joyous time of fast, let us prepare ourselves for spiritual victories, let us purify our souls, our flesh, showing restraint in our passions as well as in the food we eat, finding spiritual enjoyment in doing good, so that we might become perfect in love and be conformed to the most honourable Passion of Christ our God, and to his Resurrection, rejoicing in our souls. Your grace has shone forth, O Lord and has enlightened our souls. This pleasant time of blessing, this time of penitence.'

At every Lenten service throughout the whole Fast the prayer of St Ephraim of Syria accompanies the pilgrim people on the journey to Easter. Anyone who visits Russia will know that everyone is reared on the words of the nineteenth-century poet Alexander Puskhin. One of the great laureate's most Christian poems is a reworking of St Ephraim's prayer in verse:

Fathers in the wilderness and women beyond blame
composed spiritual prayers with which they raised
their hearts to realms above, and strengthened with praise
met the storms and battles below; but to me none has the same
mercy and healing as those words of the holy Ephraim
repeated throughout the sorrowful days of the Fast,
and, coming more and more often to my lips at the last
they fortify with mysterious power…

The prayer is said, with prostrations:

O, Lord and Master of my life, grant that I may not possess a spirit of futility, depression, love of my own importance, and of vain words. But grant to me, your slave, chastity and purity, the grace to submit my will to others, patience and love. O, Lord King, grant that I may see my own sinfulness and not judge my brother, for you are Blessed throughout all ages.

Lent is less about denial and more about affirmation, and the liturgy underlines the spiritual truth of this, for on the eve of Holy Week, the prayer is:

The forty days are accomplished and our souls have gained the benefit; and now in the holy week of your passion, O Lover of mankind, we ask to see your greatness and praise you for your immeasurable love for us…

The services in Holy Week, which begin with Palm Sunday and the commemoration of Christ's triumphant entry into Jerusalem, follow closely the events in the Gospels and are interwoven with prayers of great devotion:

O, Master, Thou hast shown Thy disciples the humility which raises us on high… Therefore, O Saviour, we cry aloud to Thee in faith. O God of our fathers, blessed art Thou.

O Zion, holy mountain of God, and Jerusalem, lift up thine eyes round about and behold thy children, gathered in thee. For, lo, they have come from afar to worship thy King. Peace be upon Israel…

I have transgressed more than the adulteress, O blessed one, yet in no wise do I bring unto Thee floods of tears. Still in silent prayer I fall down before Thee and with love embrace thy most pure feet…

I see Thy bridal chamber adorned, O my Saviour, and I have no wedding garment that I may enter there. Make the robe of my soul to shine, O Giver of Light and save me.

O Bridegroom, surpassing all in beauty, Thou hast called us to the spiritual feast of Thy bridal chamber. Strip from me the disfigurement of sin, through participation in thy sufferings, clothe me in the glorious robe of Thy beauty, and in Thy compassion make me feast with joy at Thy Kingdom…

He who clothes Himself in light as a garment, stood naked at judgment; on His cheek He received blows from the hands which He had formed… Let us worship Him…

Today He who hung the earth upon the waters is hung upon the Cross. He who is King of the angels is arrayed in a crown of thorns. He who wraps the heavens in clouds is wrapped in the purple of mockery… We venerate Thy Passion, O Christ. Show us also Thy glorious Resurrection…

From the Lenten Triodion, *Kallistos Ware*

'To praise you with pure hearts':
Easter with songs and snow

Sometimes Easter coincides with the coming of spring, when the snow has melted and the trees shake out their leaves of fresh green, but if it is earlier in April, very often there will still be snow. It was so for my first Russian Easter. It was the eve of *glasnost*, cracks were appearing in the political ice, and people were starting to crowd into church. Indeed, so great was the crowd that a guard of bouncers stood around the church I attended. Snow fell thickly on the heads and shoulders of beggars, dark shapes who weren't supposed to exist in Communist Russia, but had somehow found their way into the grounds of the church.

Crushed to one side, I saw little and understood less—and yet I caught the great drama of the resurrection as never before. The church was in darkness. Everyone, hundreds and hundreds of people, was still, expectant, hushed. Towards midnight the clergy moved in solemn procession through the crowd, out of the church, around its walls. The church was still in darkness but people held candles in readiness and now a single flame was lit, and then another, and another. People passed the light around and as the clergy returned with a great burst of acclamation: 'Christ is risen!' all the candles blazed. The choir burst into jubilant song. I knew very little Russian, and in any case they were singing in Old Church Slavonic: 'Your Resurrection, O Christ our Saviour, the angels praise in heaven, and it is fitting for us on earth to praise you with pure hearts.'

And then I heard another song. It swelled from the old women around me, the shawled *babushki* who had nothing to lose under the Soviets and even less to gain in the raw, new Russia which was about to dawn. They were the daughters and granddaughters of Leninism—and yet they caught and echoed the words the choir sang. 'To praise you with pure hearts.' I hadn't understood the words when the choir sang them, but from the constant chanting of these long-suffering women I picked them up: 'To praise you with pure hearts...' Over and over again resounded the joyous shout: 'Christ is risen!' Over and over again the cry echoed back:

'He is truly risen, he is risen indeed.' And over and over again the women of Russia sang their refrain.

Young people, their heads and shoulders covered in thick snowflakes, burst into the church—they had got through the cordon of bodyguards at last. They had perhaps never been to church before, but they too caught the great Easter acclamation, 'Christ is risen' and echoed it back: 'He is risen indeed!'

I went back to Scotland on a high with Easter. For the Easter greeting spills out into the street and into the home and people greet each other with the words which are the bedrock of our faith: Christ is risen! Truly he is risen!

Friends who have prepared together, kept the fast together, greet Easter with a whole new dimension of joy, so how much more must whole congregations? The tremendous affirmation, 'Risen indeed' resonates very deeply when the soil of our hearts has been prepared for the grain of wheat to fall and die—and live again, so that 'the little hills rejoice on every side' and valleys sing.

Chapter 6

'God's Gentle Whisper'
The Way of the Heart

Luke 2:19

*But Mary treasured up all these words
and pondered them in her heart.*

There is a great mystery in hiddenness. The first chapters of Luke's Gospel show the wonder and might of the Lord breaking into the lives of hidden people. Mary and Elizabeth met and greeted each other in secret. Their joy belonged to themselves alone—but later it was made manifest, first among the neighbours and then throughout the whole hill-country of Judea (Luke 1:65), then to the shepherds (Luke 2:8–20).

Churches in the West, on the whole, tend not to emphasize the way of being hidden. Publicity, advertising our services, costs us time and effort. We stress: 'All are welcome. Do come.' But in spite of all our efforts, fewer and fewer people come. Orthodoxy doesn't advertise. For nearly eighty years, in any case, in Russia it was forbidden. But people come and even if they don't understand what's going on they draw aside and soak up just being in the presence of God. As we have seen, the Orthodox pray with their eyes open, with all their senses alert. And there is a great drawing power in worship. The sheer delight and wonder of worship can catch people unawares and draw them into the Kingdom of God.

But in our desire to see results, we've forgotten 'the still small voice', God's 'gentle whisper' (1 Kings 19:12).

And yet, against the background of feeling failures, if we're not visibly among those who 'come home with shouts of joy, carrying their sheaves' (Psalm 126:6), people, as we have seen, are recapturing the place of retreat, the use of stillness and there are still hermits in our churches. Perhaps it is their prayers, rather than overmuch advertising, which brings souls to Christ.

Traditionalism—no; but what about tradition?

From the 1960s on, many churches in the West have made major attempts to update themselves, to make a break with old, traditional ways, to modernize their style of ecclesiastical dress and furniture, their music and so on. Preachers have always gone out to the market-place, but now it's quite common for services to be held in pubs and coffee places, stadiums and theatres. And this is well, for the church must go where people are, as Jesus did. Christ taught in the synagogue and at the lakeshore, in the temple precincts and at parties with prostitutes. George Macleod of Fuinary, founder of the Iona Community, wrote rightly that Christ was not crucified in a cathedral between two candlesticks, but on the town garbage heap, where soldiers drank and gambled and thieves cursed, a place so cosmopolitan that the sign above his cross was written in three languages.

But in trying to avoid traditionalism churches forgot tradition. There's a fine balance indeed between the two, but I detect a real movement now for people to explore the past, rediscover old prayers and music, not least the Celtic way—and the Orthodox. It may be helpful to note that Russian Orthodox thinkers call tradition 'the silence of Christ', reminding us that the Lord taught in parables to 'those on the outside' but to the apostles he said, 'The secret of the kingdom of God has been given to you' (Mark 4:11). The apostles are honoured in Orthodoxy, and to their words and works are added the lives of the saints and the teachings of the Fathers, facets of faith set fast in the Orthodox way like inclusions in amber.

Perhaps it's helpful, too, to flash back into history and recall that the period in which the Slavs were being Christianized was the time when major rifts were taking place between the Church leadership of the East and West. The conversion of the Russian people occurred just before the final breach of communion between the two halves of Christendom. The Russians were not involved in the schism, but implicit in the Russian mind-set is the idea that Rome was the centre of dangerous innovation—and that suspicion remains to this day. Eastern Christianity came to the people of Rus already formulated. It was profoundly biblical, and has remained so. The Bible has always been the basis for evangelism and for propagating dogma. Christ's command to evangelize is taken as seriously by the Orthodox as it is by any Western missionary organization:

Go therefore and make disciples of all nations, baptizing them in the name of the Father and of the Son and of the Holy Spirit, and teaching them to obey everything that I have commanded you. And remember I am with you always, to the end of the age.

(Matthew 28:19–20)

But Orthodoxy views scripture in the light of the teachings of the Church: 'teaching them to obey everything that I have commanded you' is understood to be the tradition of the Church which began with the apostles and was consolidated by the early Church councils and the Fathers. Tribes who were emerging from heathenism found this very centralized set of doctrines a very acceptable package—it is no less so for people coming from the paganism of Leninism, with its pantheon of discredited leaders.

So Orthodoxy has always been profoundly biblical, while at the same time it delights in honouring the tradition of the Church and the saints. It has been pointed out that because the ancient complaint against Rome was that it had innovated, Orthodoxy was bound to pride itself on being conservative. That doesn't mean, however, that Orthodox churches haven't split off from one another and formed 'autocephalous', independent or self-governing, churches.

It is impossible, when attending our Orthodox services, not to be moved by the Spirit…

But the bottom line is that Russians do not want to change their ancient ways, which have inspired their greatest writers, artists and musicians. In a letter written in 1877, Tchaikovsky says,

The Liturgy of St John Chrysostom is, in my view, one of the greatest artistic works. If you follow the service attentively, going carefully into the meaning of every act of the ritual, then it is impossible, when attending

our Orthodox services, not to be moved by the spirit. I also love very much the all-night vigil. To direct myself on Saturday to some small, ancient church, to stand in the semi-darkness, filled with the smoke of incense, to delve deeply within myself in search of a reply to the eternal questions: to what purpose, when, whither, why?; to waken from my reverie when the choir sings, 'Many a time have they afflicted me from my youth...' and to surrender myself to the captivating poetry of that psalm, to be filled with a certain quiet rapture when they open the central doors of the iconostasis and there rings out: 'Praise God from the heavens!' O, I love all this passionately; it is one of my great delights...

Tchaikovsky to Nadezhda von Meck December 1877, quoted
Tchaikovsky, The Crisis Years, David Brown, 1982

Thousands of contemporary Russian Christians would echo Tchaikovsky's rapturous words, not least because they are still reclaiming the old ways out of the vacuum of official atheism. Here is the testimony of two contemporary icon painters, one a monk, the other a woman.

Father Zinon

Father Zinon is a priest-monk in the monastery of Pechery, Pskov, an old town lying south-west of St Petersburg on the lake which becomes the border with Estonia. He has a simple cell with a table and wooden chair, and a studio with a view out to the blue and gold of the domes of the Church of the Dormition; in the distance the enormous golden dome of St Michael's Cathedral shines across thick foliage, which softens the landscape of Russia for such a short season of summer ease.

Father Zinon was born in 1953 (the year Stalin died) and went to art school where he began painting icons, copying the old Russian masters. Compulsory National Service followed and, incredibly, given the anti-religious propaganda of the day, the young soldier, demobbed, came to Pechery monastery. It was 1976. He made his monastic vows that same month, and took the name Zinon. He was ordained deacon and then priest-monk. His work as an artist is inextricably linked with his life as a monk. 'Icon painting is a collective endeavour,' he says. 'The primary icon painters are the Church Fathers themselves. We are simply co-authors.'

Father Zinon's name has become synonymous with the great renaissance of religious art which began in the 1980s. 'Without Father Zinon,' say his fellow artists, 'we wouldn't be painting icons. None of our work would exist at all.' He is internationally known. American and European icon painters study under him and he receives letters from all over the world. He refuses to work for money. He works for the glory of God and the only payment he asks is that people will remember him in their prayers. He has plans for the future, but for him the way forward is to go back. For Father Zinon that means back to Byzantium itself. 'We have lost too much,' he laments. 'The level of spiritual life has sunk so low that we can't look to our contemporary world for help. We need to rediscover the great secrets of icon painting, but the profound spirituality in the Russian icons of the fifteenth and sixteenth centuries is beyond our reach. So we have to do what our forebears did: study the sources. Once we have mastered the tradition we may find a vehicle for the spirit which will speak to our impoverished modern world.'

Father Zinon's work is permeated by his life of prayer, his monastic vocation, his fasting. He believes this is the only way forward for Russia. 'The word, spoken and written, has been trivialized and cheapened by mass media. It has lost its power to influence modern consciousness and reach into people's minds. Only the image can communicate spiritual unity.'

However, Father Zinon is a priest as well as a painter and people come to him for spiritual direction as well as to learn from him as an artist. His life is punctuated by long monastic services, where his spiritual children draw inspiration from his total participation in the liturgy, from the radiant look on his face as he prays. Of him it has been said, 'His heart is open to all those who are in need or suffering while the work he creates brings joy to their hearts.' (Based on an interview with Archimanrite Zinon by S.V. Timchenko in *Russian Icons Today*, Sovremennik 1994.)

'I can remember the very place where it happened':
a Russian icon painter talks of her path to faith

Another icon painter, Lyudmila Minina, grew up as an army child, moving from one military base to another. There would have been enormous disciplinary and atheistic pressures in this kind of life which must have been hard for a creative child. For Lyudmila felt the need to create very early and she both drew and wrote poetry. She graduated from Moscow Art College and went to work in the city of Kazan, painting stage sets for the theatre. After the birth of her son she went through a period of withdrawal and stayed at home, earning her living by needlework. She became interested in Eastern mysticism, the path to Christ which many young intellectuals took in Russia in those years. Her knowledge of God, of scripture, of the Church, was very vague, but when she was in her early thirties she had a sudden, direct conversion experience. 'I can remember the very place where it happened,' she says, 'the place where I felt the presence of God.'

A year later she was baptized and suddenly the great depths of the life of the spirit opened up for her. She stopped writing poetry, feeling that the Divine Liturgy has said everything that needs to be said in language more beautiful than she could achieve—and this, too, has been an experience other writers and poets have shared. Her life changed so much that she couldn't live as she had done before—and, again, one has to know the sterility and deceit of Soviet existence to be aware of the mind-blowing experience it was for so many people when they found Christ and felt the fire of the Spirit purifying and cleansing them.

It may be, however, that this kind of crisis which people went through in the 1980s under Communism is what is happening now in the commercialized, capitalistic West. Reports and statistics are given to church leaders of decline in membership, of the high proportion of elderly and even very elderly... Our churches are dying, say the statistics. Church leaders try to whip up campaigns for evangelism. Radical bishops rewrite the creeds, but many, many ordinary believers hunger for—and seek—the way of the heart.

Lyudmila sought an answer to her quest in the spiritual roots she was rediscovering in Russian Orthodoxy. She chose the way of hiddenness: she went to a monastery and sought the advice of a monk, a *staretz*, and elder—the word literally means old man, but it is understood to refer to a person who is so steeped in prayer that he or she has great wisdom and discernment and is sought out as a spiritual director. The pattern of the hermit-counsellor dates right back to the desert, and remains at the heart of Russian Orthodoxy today.

The elder listened to her story and gave her his blessing to become an icon painter. This was totally unexpected—painting icons had been something which had never occurred to her; but as she thought it over she began to realize that the elder, the *staretz*, had been used by the Holy Spirit and she had really received the blessing of the Holy Spirit for her work. From this experience she learnt to value the role of the spiritual director—a vital part of Orthodoxy. People don't meet in fellowship groups as we understand the term, but will gather around a spiritual father or mother—usually travelling great distances to do so—and, in the Communist times, taking great risks. Such people often became spiritual brothers and sisters; the flowering of religious life which burst out of its tight bonds around 1990 had been growing in the dark, in secret in the soil of the hidden life.

Lyudmila claims as a personal scripture the words of Mark 10, the healing of blind Bartimaeus: 'Jesus said to him, "What do you want me to do for you?" The blind man said to him, "My teacher, let me see again." Jesus said to him, "Go, your faith has made you well." Immediately he regained his sight and followed him on the way' (Mark 10:51–52).

Over and over again in Russia one meets people of whom it can be said that their eyes were opened and they saw and 'followed him on the way'.

Prayer: 'the true breath of the new life in Christ'

Their pilgrim way means absorbing the art of prayer, 'the true breath of the new life in Christ'. Recently I bought a small collection of Russian Orthodox prayers to be used morning and evening,

107

prayers for the sick, for the family, prayers when we travel, prayers when we work, prayers before and after meals. These prayers are woven into the life of an Orthodox believer and form the basis of the spirituality of people who live not in monasteries, but in towns and cities, in tiny cramped flats, whole families in single rooms.

Embedded among the prayers was the following small treatise which sums up volumes of Orthodox teaching distilled through the centuries. It is the essence of two great works on prayer and the spiritual life, the *Philokalia*, which has undergirded Russian prayer life since it was translated from the Greek in 1792, and *The Art of Prayer*, a much shorter anthology, the fruit of a lifetime's monastic study which draws largely on the work of two great nineteenth-century spiritual writers and was compiled in 1936 by Father Chariton, a monk in Valamo monastery in Karelia, which was shortly to be absorbed into the USSR. These books require years of prayerful study, but the following words give a summary which someone like me is more able to absorb into the routines of daily life:

Prayer is the lifting of the mind and the heart to God. It is a spiritual conversation between a human soul and the Lord. St Macarius the Great called it the chiefest of all the virtues because by prayer we obtain mercy of the Lord.

Prayer is the mother of all good deeds, a trustworthy bridge with which to traverse all kinds of temptations, a safe place of refuge, an impregnable wall for all believers, divine robes clothing the soul in great blessedness and beauty. Prayer is a sure means of defence against all attacks of our enemy, the devil. There is nothing the devils hate more than when a person submits to the cross of Christ and prays continually, day and night.

But strongest of all is the Name of Christ. The Fathers say, 'Beat down all the powers of evil with the Name of Christ. There is no stronger weapon in heaven or in earth.'

Even the holy apostles couldn't drive out unclean spirits and the Lord, the divine teacher, had to tell them somewhat sorrowfully: 'This kind does not come out except by prayer and fasting' (Matthew 17:21).

By prayer we enter the ranks of the angels and become partakers of their blessedness; we are enlightened by their wisdom. Prayer is as indispensable for the human soul as the air is for breathing or water for life. The person who doesn't pray deprives himself of fellowship with God and becomes like the dry, fruitless tree which, as the holy Gospel says, 'will be cut down and thrown into the fire' (Matthew 7:19). The person who doesn't pray cannot receive God's blessing on his or her earthly deeds. There are thousands of examples in our everyday life of how unproductive everything is which is done without the blessing of God. What God has not blessed collapses and perishes: 'Unless the Lord builds the house those that build it labour in vain' (Psalm 127:1).

It's better to sit down and think about God than stand up and think about your legs.

The teaching on the discipline of prayer is repeated again and again. One of the most enlightened and self-giving priests of recent years was Father Alexander Men, a scholar whose learning sat so lightly that he could communicate it memorably to ordinary people in ways which fitted the cramped, confused lives of Soviet citizens, a Bible teacher whose lectures lit up drab assembly rooms, inspired the Moscow intelligentsia, but was accessible to his ordinary parishioners. Amongst his many spiritual writings is a booklet on prayer, part of a major work called *Life in the Church*. Father Men was murdered early in the morning on 9 September 1990. He was hacked down with an axe as he made his way through the woods to the local railway station to catch a train to the church where he served. His killers have never been discovered, and although there is a publishing house and a university in his name, his books are not sold in official Orthodox bookshops in Russia. If you can find them at all, they tend to be in a general religious section, alongside books on Eastern mysticism, yoga and so on. Many titles seem to have disappeared altogether by a censorship of silence.

Father Alexander advised his spiritual children to learn by heart the prayers which form the basis of morning and evening worship, so that they could say them inwardly as they travelled to work, as they stood in endless queues. Like other Orthodox teachers, Father Men teaches that prayer is not a matter of saying the right words, but an attitude of mind and body, spirit and soul. 'It's not recommended to pray sitting down,' he writes sternly. 'That posture is better for prayerful meditation.' However, with the touch of humour which made his erudition so palatable, he quotes a great spiritual teacher of the nineteenth century, Metropolitan Philaret, who said, 'It's better to sit down and think about God than stand up and think about your legs.'

While there may be much external which seems to divide Christians in our way of worship, the way of the heart unites us all. Russian Orthodoxy spirituality is a missionary witness in that it invites us to claim for Christ the inner territory of the human heart which many of us find hard to let Jesus own. Here now are my translations of some of the prayers Russian Christians use in their daily lives and I include them because they are also the bedrock of our Western tradition.

Before sleep, make the sign of the cross and say: Into your hands, Lord Jesus Christ, my Lord and my God, I give my spirit. Bless me, have mercy on me and grant me eternal life. Amen.

Morning Prayer: When you awake, the teachers on prayer advise, before doing anything else at all, stand reverently, breathe evenly and slowly, so that you quiet your mind. Remind yourself that you stand before the One who sees everything, and, making the sign of the cross, say: In the Name of the Father and of the Son and of the Holy Spirit. Amen.

Now wait for a little, gathering your feelings and thoughts into quietness, not focusing on earthly things and then say the following prayers without haste and with an attentive heart:

God, have mercy on me, a sinner. (The prayer of the tax collector, Luke 18:13—this prayer should be accompanied by a low bow, touching the floor with the right hand, a physical expression of our unworthiness, our dependence on the Lord for his mercy.)

A cluster of prayers which are
basic to the Orthodox way

Lord Jesus Christ, Son of God, for the sake of the prayers of your most holy Mother and all the saints, have mercy on us. Amen.

Glory be to you, our God, glory to you.

Prayer to the Holy Spirit: Heavenly King, Comforter, Spirit of Truth, everywhere present and filling all things, Treasury of blessings and Giver of Life, come and dwell in us and cleanse us from every kind of wrong and save, O Blessed One, our souls.

To the Thrice Holy: Holy God, Holy and Strong, Holy and Immortal have mercy on us. (This prayer is said three times, making the sign of the cross and bowing from the waist.)

Glory to the Father and to the Son and to Holy Spirit, now and in the future and in all the ages to come. Amen.

Prayer to the Holy Trinity: Most Holy Trinity, have mercy on us. Lord, cleanse our sins; Master forgive our lawlessness; Holy One, visit us and heal our infirmities for your Name's sake. Lord have mercy, Lord have mercy, Lord have mercy.

Then follows the Lord's Prayer, which all Christians share.

This is the basic pattern, and most Orthodox Christians know these prayers by heart. More prayers follow; Psalm 51 is read in its entirety in Old Church Slavonic; the Nicene Creed is said, followed by prayers by the Holy Fathers, prayers for ourselves, for humility and holiness, prayers for our family, those whom we love, living and departed, for our country, its rulers and governors, for Orthodox Christians and those who have departed from the faith and are lost in heresy, and morning prayer finishes with the prayer to Christ, the Son of God, with which it was begun.

The Orthodox Fathers, however, while recommending the set prayers of the Church, don't ignore the habit of extempore prayer. If, when you are praying the set prayers, prayer starts to form itself in your own words, stay with that, they advise. The important thing is to be focused on God. Prayer is no ego trip, but the reverse. Prayer must be rooted in the love of God and of my neighbour, as the following short prayers show. They are to be said at the start of the day and they were used by the last *startzy*—elders of the hermitage of Optina, a great spiritual centre in Russia:

Lord, give me the grace to meet with a tranquil spirit all that awaits me in this new day. Lord, give me the grace to submit my whole self to your holy will. Lord, throughout every hour of this day direct and sustain me in all things.

Lord, teach me to receive with a peaceful spirit and with firm resolution whatever news I might receive this day, seeing in all things your holy will.

Lord, direct my thoughts and emotions in everything I do and say and in all unforeseen circumstances do not let me forget that everything comes from your hand.

Lord, teach me to act openly and wisely with every member of my family and with all those who are close to me, causing no one grief or sorrow.

Lord, give me strength for the coming day; and in everything which lies ahead in the course of this day direct my will and teach me to pray, to hope, to believe, to be long-suffering, to forgive and to love. Amen.

Optina Pustyn

The monastery at Optina Pustyn (*pustynia* means 'wilderness' in Russia) had an enormous impact on Russia in the nineteenth century, drawing writers and intellectuals, including Tolstoy and Dostoyevsky. The life-affirming, loving monk-counsellor in *Brothers Karamazov* is partly modelled on a *staretz*—elder of Optina, Father Amvrosy. The elders who had withdrawn from the world to join their lives to God opened themselves to people, intellectuals and peasants, army officers and merchants, women— no one was turned away. Their lives touched thousands of people and ripples continued to be felt right into the troubled twentieth century when the monastery was closed by the totalitarian regime.

> *I will bless the Lord at all times;*
> *his praise shall be continually in my mouth.* (Psalm 34:1)

The teaching of these monks, continuing the traditions of the early Fathers, is that we should pray throughout the day, before starting any action and on finishing it, before and after meals, and try to maintain a spirit of prayer, 'without ceasing'. Basing his thoughts on the apostle Paul, who says, 'persevere in prayer' (Romans 12:12) and 'pray without ceasing' (1 Thessalonians 5:17), St John Chrysostom (of the Golden Mouth) taught in the fourth century that Christians should spend set times each day in prayer: 'I call upon God and the Lord will save me. Evening and morning and at noon...' (Psalm 55:17–18).

'By constant prayer in your soul, prepare yourself for your set times of prayer and you will soon have success,' said St John Climacus, four hundred years later.

Prayer should never be mechanical, but we should endeavour to pray 'with our mind in our heart', not letting our thoughts wander but trying to concentrate on the Lord; if such attentive prayer becomes habitual we will find that our spirit has moved beyond the words of the prayer, if the Lord so leads, into a state which is prayer, yet is wordless.

This requires patience and trust: if we have messed up our time of prayer by not concentrating, then we simply have to cling even more to the mercy of God and try to do better next time. For prayer doesn't depend on our performance: it is all God's abundant mercy. 'Grace builds up everything, because grace is always present in believers. Those who commit themselves irrevocably to grace will pass under its guidance, and it shapes and forms them in a way known only to itself,' wrote St Theophan, the hermit-bishop and spiritual director to countless souls.

Constant prayer is the foundation of the monastic life, where prayer goes so deeply into the heart that it can become part of the very rhythm of the soul, waking or sleeping. It is the warp and the weft of holy scripture, not just the teaching of Paul, but of the Psalms as well: 'I will bless the Lord at all times; his praise shall be continually in my mouth' (Psalm 34:1). And writer of the Song of Songs says simply, 'I slept, but my heart was awake...' (Song of Solomon 5:2). Awake, and attentive to hear the voice of the Beloved.

Prayer indwells the soul, say the Fathers, and takes root in the heart like a bubbling fountain, continually springing up and calling to the Lord.

But although it is indispensable to monastic life, which would be pointless without it, it is also the duty of lay-people.

My brother Christians, don't think that only monks or clergy are bound to pray continually, and not lay-people. No, no, all of us Christians should constantly dwell in prayer... For when we sit down to do a piece of work or when we walk about, or when we prepare food, we can direct our thoughts to God and pray in a way which is pleasing to him... Blessed are those who become accustomed to doing this heavenly work, for they will always be conquerors, overcoming all kinds of temptation; and the dew of the Holy Spirit will fall gently in their hearts.

So wrote Gregory Palamas in the fourteenth century, and he went on:

O, there is nothing comparable to this kind of prayer! It is the light which lights up the human soul and kindles a great fire of love for God in our hearts. It is the chain which binds us to God and God to us, for it puts each person who practises it into a state of uninterrupted conversation with God. Yes, and what could you desire more than to direct your thoughts to God and mentally stand in his presence day and night, continually conversing with him—for without God there is no blessing, neither in this life nor in the next.

Prayer—'a state of uninterrupted conversation with God'

St Gregory Palamas (1296–1359) is an example of the hermit monks whose life of prayer lit a flame for other Christians. He was Greek, and had been born into a noble family. In his early twenties he entered the monastic life on Mount Athos and there he developed the practice of prayer of the heart—sitting with his head bent, his eyes focused within himself, concentrating on the heart which he longed to brim over with prayer. This form of inner prayer, based above all on the Name of Jesus, is known as *Hesychasm*, from the Greek word for quietness or repose.

Just as Andrey Rublev, a century later, painted his great icons in troubled times—and he, too, was influenced by the *Hesychast* movement—so Gregory also lived his life of prayer in the midst of turbulence and difficulty. The advance of the Turks forced him to flee to Thessalonika where he was ordained priest. He retired as a hermit, but was soon back in Mount Athos where he was caught up in theological controversy and was moved back to Thessalonika where he was consecrated archbishop in 1347. During a journey to Constantinople in 1354 he was captured by the Turks and remained in captivity for more than a year.

Gregory taught that in his incarnation Christ has sanctified the body as well as the soul. While Western monasticism majored on mortifying the flesh, Gregory and his school of *Hesychast* mystics said that emotions too have to be consecrated to God. We bring them into the stillness of the prayer of the heart, the prayer which 'puts each person who practises it into a state of uninterrupted conversation with God'.

Like the fourteenth-century writer of *The Cloud of Unknowing*, Gregory believed that God's essence remains unknowable, but that the grace of God, which permeates all things, makes God known to us.

Just as Christ was transfigured with light before three disciples only, those whose spirits are filled with the grace of uninterrupted prayer may be granted a vision of the light of Christ. This light is spiritual but it is none the less real. The light is not created, like sunlight. It is uncreated, the light of the Holy Trinity; but, stresses Gregory, it is God's glory, not his inner nature, which remains unknowable to us. 'The divine darkness is the unapproachable light in which God is said to dwell,' said Dionysius the Areopagite in the fifth century and so Gregory Palamas taught that 'by virtue of its transcendence' the light of God is experienced by us as 'darkness'.

The Jesus Prayer

The Orthodox teaching on constant prayer is a response to Paul's injunction to 'pray without ceasing'. It is built upon the regular repetition of very short phrases, usually the Jesus Prayer, which is repeated thousands of times, day and night; 'Lord Jesus Christ, Son of God, have mercy on me, a sinner!' The tradition behind this seemingly simple prayer, directed to the Lord Jesus, is rooted in holy scripture, for it is based on the insistent cry of the beggar, Bartimaeus (Luke 18:35–43). It is profoundly theological; it acknowledges the total working of the Trinity in our salvation. 'Jesus' is the name given to the Son by the Father (Luke 1:31). It is the name which describes the saving work of the Lord: 'for he will save his people from their sins' (Matthew 1:21). It is the 'name that is above every name', at which 'every knee should bend, in heaven and on earth and under the earth'; and when we confess Jesus as Lord, we do so 'to the glory of God the Father' (Philippians 2:10–11).

We also acknowledge the work of the Holy Spirit, since it is only by the Holy Spirit that we may call Jesus 'Lord' (1 Corinthians 12:3), and therefore when we pray this prayer we may be sure that the Holy Spirit, the Comforter, indwells our souls. The Jesus Prayer contains adoration and penitence, trust and devotion. It is a prayer of utmost simplicity, yet it can be the work of a lifetime too. It was rooted in the monastic life of prayer, yet it can be prayed on the top of a bus, behind a car steering-wheel in a traffic jam. It is a way which unites all Christian traditions, but although St Bernard of Clairvaux, St Francis and many other Western Christians had a great devotion to the Holy Name of Jesus, the Jesus Prayer only became known in the West after the Russian revolution, with the scattering of Russian émigrés who brought little with them—but brought their great spiritual tradition. The *Philokalia* and other spiritual works were translated into English in the 1930s and gradually people became familiar with the Jesus Prayer. But the Russian writers stress that the prayer is only an aid, a help. It is a means to an end, not an end in itself. 'If you limit your prayer to words only, you are a "sounding brass" (1 Corinthians 13:1),' warns Bishop Theophan the Recluse. 'The prayer, "Lord Jesus Christ, Son of

God, have mercy on me" is an oral prayer like any other. There is nothing special about it in itself, but it receives all its power from the state of mind in which it is made... The Jesus Prayer is a good means to arrive at inner prayer, but in itself it is not inner but outer prayer... everything depends on conscious and free turning to God, and on a balanced effort to hold oneself in him.'

These words of Theophan are quoted in the personal anthology of Father Chariton of Valamo monastery, *The Art of Prayer*, and Theophan also warns us that 'the Jesus Prayer is not some talisman. Its power comes from faith in the Lord and from deep union of the mind and heart with Him... a mere repetition of the words does not signify anything.'

Theophan was the son of a parish priest whose heart always lay in the life of prayer and hiddenness. He was ordained priest after study at the Theological Academy in Kiev and later became professor at the Theological Academy in St Petersburg. He also served in the Middle East and in Palestine and was destined for a brilliant career in the Church, being made rector of the St Petersburg Academy, and, in 1859, he was consecrated as a bishop. But in 1866 he gave up public service and retired to a monastery where, after six years of taking a full part in all the monastic prayers and services, he entered strict enclosure, seeing no one except his spiritual father and the superior of the monastery. He lived in two small, poorly furnished rooms with a little chapel, which was also poorly appointed. Highly educated, he retained a well-stocked library and divided his time between prayer, the study of the Fathers and an enormous correspondence, mainly with women. For relaxation he did carpentry and painted icons. He lived austerely, his daily diet was a glass of tea and bread, morning and evening, with an egg if it was not a fast day.

Theophan lived like this for almost three decades, until his death, and it is some of the writings from his vast correspondence, which ran to ten volumes, that Father Chariton included in *The Art of Prayer*. Erudite, austere, ascetic, totally enclosed, Theophan was a warm, loving man with a great gift of imparting knowledge with charm and immediacy. To him, and to a little classic on Orthodox prayer called *The Way of a Pilgrim*, which charts the spiritual progress of a simple Christian who wanders through Russia praying the Jesus Prayer and living on the mercy of the Lord, people like me owe an understanding of the depth and energy of prayer. 'Prayer is the test of everything; prayer is also the source of everything; prayer is the driving force of everything. If prayer is right, everything is right. For prayer will not allow anything to go wrong,' writes St Theophan. But he warns that it is hard work. 'At first this saving prayer [the Jesus Prayer] is usually a matter of strenuous effort and hard work. But if one concentrates on it with zeal, it will begin to flow of its own accord, like a brook that murmurs to the heart. This is a great blessing and it is worth working hard to obtain it.'

The unknown pilgrim worked hard: his *staretz*-elder advised him to recite the Prayer three thousand times a day, then six thousand times, finally twelve thousand times—after which the Prayer becomes part of his being and he can stop counting.

And that is how I go about now, and ceaselessly repeat the Prayer of Jesus, which is more precious and sweet to me than anything in the world. At times I do as much as forty-three or forty-four miles a day, and do not feel that I am walking at all, I am aware only of the fact that I am saying my Prayer. When the bitter cold pierces me, I begin to say my Prayer more earnestly, and I quickly become warm all over. When hunger begins to overcome me, I call more often on the name of Jesus and I forget my wish for food. When I fall ill and get rheumatism in my back and legs I fix my thoughts on the Jesus Prayer, and do not notice the pain. If anyone harms me, I only have to think, 'How sweet is the Prayer of Jesus!' and the injury and the anger alike pass away and I forget it all... I thank God that I now understand the meaning of those words I heard in the Epistle—'Pray without ceasing' (1 Thessalonians 5:17).

The Way of a Pilgrim, *trans. R.M. French, 1954*

Incidentally, this practice of being a wanderer for God used to be a great part of Orthodox spirituality until the revolution, when it became a crime to be a vagrant. People who took literally the words of Hebrews 13:14—'for here we have no lasting city, but we are looking for the city that is to come'—didn't fit the strict registration requirements of the police state, were arrested and sent off to labour camp.

However, all writers on prayer warn that while all Christians may use the Jesus Prayer as part and parcel of our daily walk with the Lord, a commitment to intensive use of the Prayer should be undertaken only with the blessing and guidance of a spiritual director. They also stress that a pattern of words can never be an end in itself: the aim of all prayer is to unite mind and heart in the endless love of the triune God. 'Let us run with perseverance the race that is set before us, looking to Jesus, the pioneer and perfecter of our faith...' Hebrews 12:2 is the essence of the life of prayer in Eastern and Western Christianity.

CHAPTER 7

'The Mother of My Lord...'
THE PLACE OF MARY IN
THE ORTHODOX TRADITION

LUKE 1:46, 49

*And Mary said, 'My soul magnifies the Lord... for the Mighty
One has done great things for me, and holy is his name.'*

The tradition of prayer, the way of the heart, the Jesus Prayer
which we charted in the last chapter is one which all who love the
Lord can identify with. But when it comes to his mother, some of
us run into problems. For a start, what do we call her? It felt a bit
casual simply to write 'Mary' at the beginning of this chapter. But
I didn't want to write 'The Virgin Mary' because, although the
Orthodox do refer to her in that way, the aspect they stress is not
so much the virginity of Mary, unquestioned though that is, but
her motherhood. And not in some vague way of giving a deferen-
tial nod to mothers as a whole, but specifically to Mary as the
mother of the Lord Jesus Christ, the Son of God, the second person of the Trinity, who is God. The apostles, we all agree, openly
preached Jesus, the crucified and risen Saviour: 'Repent and be
baptized every one of you in the name of Jesus Christ so that your
sins may be forgiven; and you will receive the gift of the Holy
Spirit' (Acts 2:38). The place of Mary, however, remains a hidden
one, but she certainly belonged to the little group of believers who
made up the very first Church, which took very seriously its duty
to provide for the needs of widows (Acts 6:1; James 1:27).

Even in the agony of his death, the Lord Jesus was not un-
mindful of his mother, but gave her into the care of the apostle
John—and hence, we may assume (and the Orthodox certainly
teach) of the Church. 'When Jesus saw his mother and the disciple whom he loved standing beside her, he said to his mother,

121

"Woman, here is your son." Then he said to the disciple, "Here is your mother." And from that hour the disciple took her into his own home' (John 19:26–27). These last words repay reflection. Might I, too, not offer hospitality to the mother of the Lord, not in any way exalting her as the queen of heaven, but simply offering her a place in my thoughts, taking time to study the scriptures concerning her, to meditate upon her faith, her largely hidden life, this young Jewish Miriam, who bore so gladly the great burden of salvation which prophets had foretold—and before which these grown men had quailed. There are legends in the Irish and Scots Gaelic tradition about Bride, the foster mother who helped fugitive Mary tend her infant son. My awareness of Mary in the Jesus story, however, effectively stopped with that moment in John's Gospel. I know, of course, that she is mentioned in the first chapter of the Acts, named, along with the apostles and 'certain women': 'All these were constantly devoting themselves to prayer, together with certain women, including Mary the mother of Jesus, as well as his brothers' (Acts 1:14). By implication, therefore, Mary and those other women were also with the apostles and other believers:

When the day of Pentecost had come, they were all together in one place. And suddenly there came a sound like the rush of a violent wind, and it filled the entire house where they were sitting. Divided tongues, as of fire, appeared among them and a tongue rested on each of them. All of them were filled with the Holy Spirit and began to speak in other languages, as the Spirit gave them ability.

(Acts 2:1–4)

The tradition would not, I think, say that the Spirit had rested upon any other than the twelve apostles, but it certainly accords Mary a continuing place of prayerful influence in the early Church. The Council of Ephesus in AD431, which defined Jesus as the incarnate Son of God, also established the tradition of naming Mary as 'the mother of God'. Luke's Gospel tells us that the Lord was obedient to his earthly parents (Luke 2:51). In John's Gospel we read that he performed the first saving sign of his adult ministry at his mother's request (John 2:1–11). All the most ancient Christian traditions are alike in according respect to Mary. Perhaps, after all, it is we who, in reaction to mariolatry, have failed to see what the apostles saw: that Christ loved his mother and respected her and that she, apart from one incident in which her faith failed her (Mark 3:21, 31–34), honoured him and followed him to his appalling death. Peter's faith failed him too and so did Thomas's but we haven't censored them out of our Christian story in the way we have done with Mary.

Here are two examples from the reflections of children which show us that the Orthodox teaching of Mary has in fact led these girls to a deeper understanding of the saving work of Christ:

Not long ago I acted the part of the Virgin Mary in a play. I liked doing it so much that I kept on with the part even when the play was over. My friends knelt down in front of me and I made it appear that I was forgiving their sins. But then I discovered that the Virgin Mary didn't think of herself as being holy in any way and after the death of Christ she was afraid that people would ask her to heal them, knowing she was his mother. And so I felt ashamed and I asked God to forgive me.

Another girl added:

I am amazed at the humility with which the Virgin Mary accepted and fulfilled the will of God. She wasn't afraid to be rejected by everyone. Bearing Jesus, she knew she would only give birth to the child and bring him up, but that thereafter he wouldn't need her. Jesus said, 'Whoever does the will of God is my brother and sister and mother' (Mark 3:35).

We have seen that the icons always depict the mother of God of mercy and lovingkindness showing her child to the world, pointing away from herself to the Christ... Woven into the liturgy are prayers and hymns to the Virgin in her role as the mother of God, *Bogomater*, or by the Russian translation of her Greek name, *Theotokos*, the God-bearer—*Bogoroditza*. As such she comes close to the Russian earth and the people, for Russia, Holy Russia of the saints and tsars was also the God-bearer, mystically carrying the life of God on her suffering breast.

Perhaps a help to understanding of Mary, the mother of the Lord, is the role of the Queen Mother in Britain and the respect that older people, especially, pay her. I also find it helpful to recall the splendour and rigidity of the court at Byzantium and think of the role the Emperor's mother must have played. A suit with her was a way in to the Emperor. Her deeds of piety brought honour to her son. It was a Byzantine Empress, Helena, the Queen Mother of the day, who, in the fourth century, made pilgrimages to Jerusalem so popular—an unbroken tradition for Christians of all denominations to this day.

---

*Why has this happened to me
that the mother of my Lord should come to me?* (Luke 1:43)

I go back to the Gospel of Luke, to that joyful meeting between two women, Mary and Elizabeth, both with child. 'Why has this happened to me that the mother of my Lord should come to me?' asked the aged Elizabeth (Luke 1:43).

Housebound, very aware of gossip and stares whenever she, so long barren, left her seclusion for some necessary errand, Elizabeth must have felt perplexed during the long months of her pregnancy. She must have wondered why the grace of God had touched her, what manner of child she would bear. Her husband could give her no answers—he was dumb.

I imagine Elizabeth pushing back her greying hair with a heavy hand, weary with the weight of her pregnancy, with the heat. Then suddenly at her unvisited threshold… light footsteps, a young girl's joyful voice—and Elizabeth feels the child within her leap with joy; and she is filled with the Holy Spirit.

I sense something of the joy and mystery of that meeting in the way the Orthodox honour Mary, even if I can't quite get into the sense of relationship with Mother Mary as my friends do. A friend of mine who visited Scotland confessed later that she felt sad at the way Christians she met ignored the role the Virgin Mary played in the story of our salvation. My friend felt that we were downplaying something very important and hence missing out on an important stream of spirituality. And it has to be said that this is a major barrier for many of the Orthodox who are, frankly, shocked at the impiety of not honouring the mother of God and the saints.

My husband and myself experienced this often in Russia. It became a big issue in attempts to dialogue with students in the Orthodox theological seminary in St Petersburg. I have to say that a lot of the barrier-making came from the students. On one occasion my husband was asked to speak about Anglicanism at the *diakonia* course—a kind of pastoral course at which a non-Orthodox, in theory, might just about be tolerated. Women attended the lecture too; they study icon painting and music. Women may now lead singing in churches—a fairly recent concession—and, of course, doing good works, teaching children, setting up centres for orphans and so on are also encouraged and women take an active part in these areas.

The lecture hall was full, but I noticed that many students did their own thing, women knitted, men got on with other work, even while the guest lecturer was speaking. At the end there was an opportunity for discussion. But it was stymied immediately by two questions from the floor. 'Do you honour the saints?' And, 'What is the position of the Virgin Mary?'

In Orthodoxy the position of Mary is exalted and lyrical, homely and intimate. At every church wedding in Russia, at the end of the festive service, the bride is given an icon of the mother of God, her husband is given an icon of the Saviour. Mary is the 'daughter' of Psalm 45, the 'bride of the King'. The Psalmist recites the praises of the king, but also addresses the 'daughter' who is asked to 'consider and incline your ear...' (v. 10). Mary is asked to do exactly this when the angel appears to her, for then salvation of humankind depends on the free assent of a young, unmarried girl.

Mary is 'all glorious within', which the Russian translation, as in the King James Version, allows us to make this a reference to her heart, her spiritual nature, while modern translations take the reading to be 'within her chamber' (v. 12).

Because she takes into her womb the Lamb of God, the Shepherd of the sheep, Mary is the sheepfold wherein the flock safely gathers; she is the New Testament equivalent of the pillar of cloud and fire which guided the Israelites. The Holy Spirit will come upon the unwedded girl (a person of no significance in the culture of the day); the power of the Most High will overshadow her (Luke 1:35), therefore the child to be born will be 'holy; the Son of God' (v. 36). In the Old Testament the cloud was the sign of the Lord's presence with his people (Exodus 24:15–18). Mary is seen as the Ark of the New Covenant; and when she is joyously received by her older kinswoman, the unborn child, who is the forerunner, 'leaps'—just as David had leapt and danced before the Ark (1 Chronicles 15:25–29).

Mary is not named among the women at the tomb. She is, however, seen as the one who bridges the Old Testament and the New. Her song of praise and prophecy stands directly in the Jewish tradition: God has helped his people Israel 'in remembrance of his mercy according to the promise he made to our ancestors, to Abraham and his descendants forever' (Luke 2:54–55). Mary declares explicitly that all the great reversals of power and authority which Jesus will embody are now fulfilled (vv. 51–53). The tiny body of the Saviour of the world is woven and knit together in Mary's womb, but she herself is born not of any immaculate conception but, in Orthodox tradition, to elderly, hitherto childless parents, devout Jews, who awaited the coming of the Messiah, rich in faith, poor in all else. She is mortal and dies, but, in Orthodoxy, her body is taken up into heaven (the event is celebrated by the Festival of the Dormition, or falling asleep of the Virgin Mary). Thus Mary anticipates the general resurrection of all believers which is the hope and fulfilment of the gospel (1 Corinthians 15).

In the Orthodox liturgy Mary is the star which presages the morning, she is the dawn of a sacramental day. She heals the tears of Eve. Above all, standing at the cross, watching the sufferings of her Son in humble submission, Mary, whose soul was pierced (Luke 2:35) is known in Orthodoxy as 'the joy of the sorrowful' who pray:

Watching the stream of your Son's Blood pouring forth on the cross for our salvation, you humbly submitted to the will of the Father in heaven like a slave of the Lord. You give us a picture of long-suffering and endurance, so may we, tempted in the fire and need of our earthly life sing humbly to God, alleluia.

Litany to the God-bearing Mother

Rejoice, favoured one! The Lord is with you. (Luke 2:28)

We have seen that the icons never present Mary on her own, but always show Mary with the Child, except, obviously, in the icons of the annunciation in which she is shown along with the angel. In Western Christianity, hymns and poems about the annunciation tend to form part of our services of 'lessons and carols' at Christmas, and the actual Feast of the Annunciation on 25 March gets little general attention. In Orthodoxy the event is commemorated by a major festival. The liturgy that day expresses deep joy: the Old Testament promises are fulfilled by the incarnation of the redeemer of the world. The prayer of the day says: 'Today the Son of God becomes the Son of the Virgin, and Gabriel announces the good tidings of grace. Wherefore let us also with him cry to the mother of God: Rejoice, favoured one, the Lord is with you.'

In the icons this joy is shown by the use of colour and by the posture of the figures. Gabriel is often shown with one wing raised, symbol of flight. The angel hastens swiftly into the house with the same joy of which we read in Isaiah, 'How beautiful on the mountains are the feet of those who bring good news... (52:7). He holds a staff, the symbol of a messenger, and his right hand is held towards the Virgin as he communicates the divine message to her. She is looking upwards, attentive to the command of her King. She is often shown with a scroll, or spinning red yarn.

The coming of the angel, the transmission of Blessed News, as the feast is called in Russian (*Blagoveshchenie*) is a joyous, festive occasion, but the icon painters also show the inner significance of the event: the Virgin is rendered with great restraint. Mary is perturbed. She is fearful of these extraordinary words: how shall this be? she wonders. We see this by the way she holds her hand before her breast, a slightly self-defensive gesture, the palm is upwards, showing her perplexity. We read in Matthew 1:18–20:

Now the birth of Jesus the Messiah took place in this way. When his mother Mary had been engaged to Joseph, but before they lived together, she was found to be with child from the Holy Spirit. Her husband Joseph, being a righteous man and unwilling to expose her to public disgrace, planned to dismiss her quietly. But just when he had resolved to do this, an angel of the Lord appeared to him in a dream...

Miriam was a child of the covenant and knew that her 'yes' to the angel could cost her very dearly...

As the poor and faithful of Israel had said 'Yes' to God in anguish of spirit, not seeing how things would work out but conscious only of the tearing away from what had gone before and the venture forward into the dark unknown at God's word, so Mary was being asked to make the leap of faith in response to God's self-offer and invitation. There were no models for understanding, no comforting precedents, because this thing had never happened before...

Like the prophets and the anonymous believers before her, she let go of familiar, intelligible patterns and ways of relating to God and the universe... She said her 'Yes' to the Beyond, she let go of her securities, faced the misunderstanding, bore the shame, accepted her own bewilderment and risk... There was joy for her, and in newness of life she danced with the Beyond that was within.

These words of Maria Boulding from her book *The Coming of God* (1982) did much to prepare me for the spirituality the icon painters would open up for me. Dame Maria explores Mary's place among the '*anawim*, the poor of the Lord', expounding Zephaniah 3:12: 'For I will leave in the midst of you a people humble and lowly. They shall seek refuge in the name of the Lord—the remnant of Israel.' The true Israel, that is, the faithful ones who never lost hope that the great promises of God would be fulfilled. Like Zechariah and Elizabeth, who were 'righteous before God, living blamelessly according to all the commandments and regulations of the Lord' (Luke 1:6), Mary hoped for the great moment of which Isaiah speaks: 'See, the Lord comes with might, and his arm rules for him; his reward is with him, and his recompense before him. He will feed his flock like a shepherd, he will gather the lambs in his arms, and carry them in his bosom and gently lead the mother sheep' (Isaiah 40:10–11). Power and tenderness: the fulfilment of both rested now with her. Dare she refuse the one who comes? Dare she agree to bear in her womb the one who gently leads the *gravid*, those who are big with child?

Then Mary said, 'Here I am, the servant of the Lord; let it be with me according to your word.' (Luke 2:37)

The culminating moment comes with the submission of Mary, and some icons focus on this. Bowing her head, she presses her right hand to her breast—the gesture of acceptance which has decided the fate of the world. 'In the days of the creation of the world, when God was uttering his living and mighty, "Let there be...", the word of the Creator brought creatures into the world,' said one of the great spiritual figures of the nineteenth century, Metropolitan Philaret, in a sermon on the Feast of the Annunciation in Moscow in 1874. 'But on that day, unexampled in the life of the world, when the Divine Miriam uttered her brief and obedient, "So be it," I hardly dare say what happened—the word of the creature brought the Creator down into the world' (quoted, *The Meaning of Icons*, Ouspensky and Lossky).

That overpowering moment has been the theme of writers and painters ever since Luke penned the words of his Gospel. The icon painters are concerned to show us that this scene is overshadowed by the presence of the Most High—the angel and the Virgin both look upwards to the partially exposed circle from which pour the descending rays of the Holy Spirit.

The icons are totally in harmony with the gospel events: the angel announces the news, the young woman freely consents to bear the Son, the Holy Spirit descends, and the Father sends his favour from on high. God's will is freely received by the Virgin. The movement of her body is directed not towards the angelic messenger but to the sender of the message. She surrenders herself to God's will. As we 'read' the icon we see the voluntary participation of the mother of Jesus in the work of salvation, and it is this primarily which Orthodoxy honours.

In this chapter, as in the rest of the book, I have endeavoured to give what I perceive as the Orthodox view, although I come from a somewhat different background. I focus with confidence on the teaching of Mary which is absolutely biblical; I draw much support from contemplating some of the icons; I have learnt to appreciate the part in our salvation which Mary played in her all-important 'yes'; I'm certain the saints in heaven still carry on the work of intercession as well as praise (Revelation 5:8–9) and that Mary does too, not least because we see her devoting herself to prayer in the beginning of Acts. My own prayer, however, must remain God-directed, Jesus-focused, and I can't quite get into that extra dimension of honour which is part of Orthodox and Roman Catholic prayer.

An icon in Vologda, an old Russian town

However, one portrayal of the Mother and Child particularly haunts me. It's an icon I came across in an old Russian town, Vologda. Tucked away in forests due east of St Petersburg, due north of Moscow, Vologda has largely missed the attention of the wider world. Its heyday was in the sixteenth century and its great cathedral, under restoration when I visited, about to be used again as a place of worship, dates from the days when English merchants brought trade and wealth to the city. John Hasse, an agent of the Moscovy Shipping Company, reported that Vologda was a good place to build warehouses in. It was conveniently placed on the banks of the River Vologda within easy reach of Moscow and Novogorod. Ivan the Terrible paid the town a visit and actually thought about making his capital here, but a tile slipped down from the cathedral roof as he passed by. He took this as a bad omen and chose Moscow instead.

After that not too much happened in Vologda. A bit of building went on in the eighteenth and nineteenth century and Lenin's sister was exiled here for a spell. It is still a centre for lacemaking, woodcarving and silver and metal work. The most recent news I had of Vologda was that school teachers there haven't been paid for over a year.

Vologda has a very fine museum, however, rich in folk crafts from the whole region and a very fine display of icons, mostly sixteenth century. I find it hard to view icons in museums. They are vehicles of prayer, not of the history of art, and I tend to hurry away from the sad, solemn gaze of the saints.

One icon in particular riveted me. It is very ancient, early four-teenth century, perhaps linked to the Tver school, but it is called The Virgin *Podkubenskaya*, so named because it was found in the town of Podkubenskoye near Vologda in the nineteenth century. It is timeless and awesome, the head and shoulders of the Child Jesus and his mother. The wood is gashed the length of the icon, cutting across the edge of the mother's left eye, the child's fore-head and cheek. The paint is yellow, the colours sombre, but the hallmark of the icon is its overpowering love. The mother wears a dark veil, deep brown and burgundy in hue, edged with a lighter burnishing which frames her face and neck. The child's cheek is curved up against his mother's. His hands hold on to her, the fin-gers curled trustingly about the edgings of her veil. But even so his gaze goes upward and outward. Her gaze is within. She is utterly still, totally at peace, but her eyes reflect great suffering. There is foreknowledge in her gaze and it is the knowledge of the cross.

This icon belongs to the very great traditions of the sacred art of old Russia. It had no place as an object in a museum. The old women of Volgda must have thought so too: they come from churches sad with dereliction, where prayers are said and candles are lit among scaffolding and mould, and make their way to the museum to continue their prayers in front of this trusting child and tender mother. I could understand them. Those huge, oriental eyes were utterly compelling. I didn't want to go away. It wasn't likely that I'd visit Vologda again, and I didn't think I'd ever find a copy of the icon.

And amazingly I did! Tucked away on a shelf in a bookshop in St Petersburg was an illustrated history of Vologda, and even though it had a definite pre-*glasnost* slant to it, it included a pho-tograph of the icon. I immediately bought the book. But icons don't belong in books either. Probably illicitly, I colour-photo-copied the photograph and had it mounted on wood. I have it in front of me as I write.

I don't know what has happened to the original icon. Perhaps when the cathedral in Vologda was finally restored, the ancient painting of the mother and her child, so alive with love and compassion, was at last returned to the courts of prayer and praise. 'Surely,' prophesied young Mary, the womb within her quick with small stirrings of life which will bring Life to the world, 'surely all generations will call me blessed; for the Mighty One has done great things for me, and holy is his name' (Luke 2:48–49).

CHAPTER 8

THE COMMUNION OF SAINTS

REVELATION 8:4

*And the smoke of the incense, with the prayers of the saints,
rose before God from the hand of the angel.*

In the Gospel stories I learn much from Mary of Bethany, who sat
at the feet of the Lord while her sister was much busied with serving (Luke 10:38–42); I may also learn from Mary the mother of
Jesus much that has been lost by an under-emphasis of her role,
which came about in reaction to pre-Reformation worship. But
what about the saints? They are certainly part of our tradition, East
and West. We have seen the significance of the texts from
Revelation—the whole company of heaven honours the Lamb and
the one who sits upon the throne (Revelation 5:7). This includes
those who suffered for their faith. They have been largely forgotten
in the West, a few legends and stories, names of churches and
people, place names remain. Not so in Russia, where the icons
portray their living presences and where people now are recapturing the custom of 'name's day'—honouring the saint whose name
you bear. That's why there are so few girls' names in Russia. Maria
(Masha), Anna, Lidia, Olga, Natalia (Natasha), Tatiana (Tanya),
Galina, Nadezhda (Nadya)—'Hope', Sophia (Sonia)—and you
soon exhaust the list because, apart from a phase in Soviet Russia
of calling people after their leaders: Svetlana (Stalin's daughter),
Leonid (Brezhnev), even Vladilen (a compound of Vladimir Illych
Lenin), and—horrors!—Electrosila (electric power), names are
supposed to be Christian; and people acknowledge their personal
saint in their prayers.

You have wounded me with your love and transformed me.

Among manifold saints of Russia, I want to highlight only two,
St Sergius of Radonezh (c. 1314–92), and St Seraphim of Sarov
(1759–1833).

St Sergius of Radonezh

Trust in the Lord, and do good; so you will live in the land, and enjoy security. Take delight in the Lord, and he will give you the desires of your heart. (Psalm 37:3–4)

Visitors to Moscow will be aware that around Moscow there is a group of ancient cities known as the Golden Ring. These include the city of Vladimir and the Holy Trinity Monastery at Zagorsk (the Soviet name for the old town). The golden domes of the monastery complex, the bell towers and great high walls of its *kremlin* (citadel) gleam in the sun. It is a place of such power and importance that it stayed open all through the Communist times: in total opposition to the mind-set enforced by the leaders in Moscow, men still took monastic vows there, donned the hair shirt and the black robes marked with a cross and the words, 'I bear in my body the marks of the Lord Jesus' (Galatians 6:17).

The town of Zagorsk has returned to its pre-revolutionary name, Sergiev Posad—the settlement of Sergei (Sergius)—and the monastery remains the spiritual centre of Russia.

There's a sense that this imposing set of buildings is to St Sergius Radonezh what the vast basilica of Assisi is to St Francis. For Sergius, who was born as Bartholomew to noble parents, lived as a hermit in utmost simplicity, building little huts in forest clearings in the heart of a Russia still enslaved by Tartar-Mongolian overlords. Drawn to his gospel life of freedom, joy and radiance, others joined him. It was out of this cluster of huts and a small wooden church dedicated to the Holy Trinity that the great monastery, still a centre of spiritual power, arose.

The kingdom of heaven is like a mustard seed that someone took and sowed in his field; it is the smallest of all the seeds, but when it has grown it is the greatest of shrubs and becomes a tree, so that the birds of the air come and make nests in its branches. (Matthew 13:31)

The parable of Jesus, surely one of the shortest stories ever told, speaks of the growth which comes from hidden things if they are in the will of God. But Sergius having found the 'hidden treasure' of prayer, the pearl of such value that a men will sell all that they have to own it (vv. 44, 45), kept seeking the life of a solitary. He would move on again to somewhere more isolated, and again others would join him. The community which formed around him begged him to become their abbot, but when his own brother, who had shared the hermit life with him, criticized his lifestyle, Sergius simply withdrew further into the forest. And again, others sought him out for prayer and advice and Sergius was reinstated as abbot while his brother went off to a more normal monastery! In this way, while never seeking fame or limelight, Sergius became the founder of a network of monastic communities which, in his lifetime and in the years following his death, spread across the whole of north Russia, while the first of them all, the Holy Trinity monastery which grew out of his small wooden church, helped to establish Moscow as the new capital of Russia. Fifty such communities were founded in his own lifetime, forty more by his followers in the next generation.

It has to be remembered that this was pioneer work: these monks built their settlements among pagan people, opening up new fields for the gospel. They were to the Russia of the fourteenth and fifteenth centuries what Columba and his Irish monks had been to Scotland in the sixth century, spreading the gospel but also cultivating virgin forest, spreading literacy, art, education— and the Russian language right to the edges of the Arctic Circle.

Do not worry about your life, what you will eat or what you will drink, or about your body, what you will wear. Is not life more than food, and the body more than clothing? (Matthew 6:25)

Sergius lived a life of prayer and hard labour, wresting rather less than subsistence living from the forest around him. He was nearly always short of food but no matter how little food they had, nor how hardly they had come by it, Sergius and his monks were always hospitable, never turning away anyone who came to them.

In the story of Christianity it seems to be that the closer people come to God, the more their inner peace and love is reflected out to the world around them—to animals as well as to the quarrelsome souls of potentates, and the troubled hearts of the poor. So Sergius habitually shared his bread—his only food—with a wild bear which came to him from the forest—and when there was not enough for both of them, he gave his share to the bear. His brothers remonstrated with him, but Sergius replied mildly, 'The beast does not know about fasting.'

Not surprisingly, people were drawn to the love they saw in him, their peasant monk who so visibly radiated the life of the Spirit and lived in joy and peace with wild beasts. The apostle Paul writes that creation itself 'waits in eager longing for the revealing of the children of God' (Romans 8:19) and Sergius' biographer, Epiphanius the Most Wise (whom we met already, writing of Andrey Rublev), commented, '...it should be known with certainty that when God dwells in a man and the Holy Spirit rests on him, all is subject to him as all was subject in the beginning to Adam, before the transgression of God's commandment...'

It seems that far from being a navel-gazing exercise of personal salvation, the choice of a life lived outright for Christ acts as a focus for reconciliation in the world. The psalmist says, 'Trust in the Lord, and do good; so you will live in the land, and enjoy security. Take delight in the Lord, and he will give you the desires of your heart... He will make your vindication shine like the light, and the justice of your cause like the noon-day' (Psalm 37:3–6). Important people started to come to the Abbot for blessing and advice. Against his will, Sergius became a prominent and influential person, totally revitalizing the spiritual life of Russia, re-establishing places of community in a war-torn land, stopping no less than four civil wars, inspiring and encouraging people to live with dignity, not as slaves of their overlords. In fact almost all the prominent people of the day, prince or abbot, duke or saint, monk or missionary were his disciples, friends or correspondents, but he never 'lost the common touch' and always stayed close to the poor.

The Orthodox historian and theologian, Kallistos Ware, has said that it was not accidental that the first monastery which grew up round Sergius is dedicated to the Holy Trinity—for the unity of the Trinity is the model for the peace and harmony which a monastery should embody in the world. Sanctity and citizen life, prayer and the great flowering of Russian icon painting are all directly linked to the hermit life of St Sergius, which spread ripples of holiness and vitality across Russia at that most difficult time. Andrey Rublev painted his famous icon of the Holy Trinity for the monastery: perhaps the charity and self-giving courtesy of the triune God so profoundly depicted in the Rublev icon mirrored the love he saw in Abbot Sergius who undertook the most lowly tasks in the monastery, delighting to till the soil of the monastery garden. 'Let the same mind be in you that was in Christ Jesus who... humbled himself and became obedient to the point of death—even death on a cross' (Philippians 2:5, 8). It is exactly this quality of life which should be the hallmark of Christian community and Sergius was a fine example of self-effacing humility. He always wore threadbare, patched clothes, shocking people who flocked to meet the famous Abbot. 'I came to see a prophet, and you show me a beggar...' one of his visitors protested.

St Sergius influenced the political life of Russia enormously: he was a close friend of the Grand Dukes of Moscow, and his personal example and the communities he founded paved the way towards a united country which discovered new strength to defend itself against its enemies. Prince Dimitry of Don—the Robert the Bruce of his day—sought out Sergius and asked for his blessing to do battle with the Tartars. Sergius blessed the Prince and predicted his victory at the Battle of Kulikovo in 1380, the Bannockburn of Russian history, which began the liberation of Russia after two hundred years of virtual slavery.

Something of the power of this came home to me a few years ago. I had gone with a group of school children from St Petersburg, not to the Golden Ring, but to a smaller, less lavish group of old Russian cities on the banks of the Volga River: Yaroslavl, Rostov Veliki—birthplace of St Sergius—and Kostroma, also closely associated with the saint. The group includes the town of Rybinsk, home of the original Volga boatmen, and Uglich, scene of the assassination of the Tsar Dmitry by Boris Gudonov in the seventeenth century, the subject of the opera by Mussorgsky. People who travel by boat along the Volga will pass Uglich.

On Orthodox Christmas Eve the children, their teachers and I caught a local train from Yaroslavl to Rostov. After the tower blocks of St Petersburg these old Russian towns seemed more manageable and human. I was particularly attracted to Rostov, whose complex of seventeenth-century walls, Bishop's palace (now a museum), winter and summer churches and enormous bell-tower were being massively restored.

Rostov is also the centre for the art of *finift*, the delicate painting on enamel which may adorn a priest's crown, a Bible cover, icons, jewellery; but special place is given to St Sergius. He is depicted on frescoes, on embroidered icons where real hair is used to make his beard. I found the icon of St Sergius, with his arresting gaze, overpowering; overpowering, too, was a low basement room filled with fourteenth- and fifteenth-century icons, too full of spirituality to have been imprisoned here. I turned away from these awesome presences with their unspoken challenge and pored over a large nineteenth-century illustrated life of St Sergius. The page was open at an engraving showing Prince Dimitry coming to the holy man to ask for his blessing. The prince kneels, and I recalled the Roman centurion who said to Jesus, 'Lord... I do not deserve to have you come under my roof... But say the word and my servant will be healed. For I myself am a man under authority, with soldiers under me...' (Luke 7:6–9). The Gospel verse became very real as I contemplated the picture of secular power which was not too proud to acknowledge the authority of God. I contrasted that with the destruction which has been wrought in Russia for the last eighty years by men who declared the State atheist and made themselves gods, plunging the country into crime, chaos and despair. In Rostov, in the room dedicated to the life of St Sergius, I saw the heart of Russia, which was not merely historic but holy—and it was extremely powerful.

For Sergius, the fruit of giving up self-will was holiness and liberty. He embodied 'the glorious freedom of the children of God' (Romans 8:21). He renounced the world—and yet he is known as the 'builder of Russia'. He enabled his defeated country to resist and conquer the conquerors. He pushed out the boundaries of Russia geographically and spiritually—for through his own deep life of prayer he strengthened the inner life of the Russian church. We have already seen that from the earliest days Christians experienced a tension between the needs of the organization, the

Church, and the divine madness of the desert which feeds the soul. St Sergius managed to maintain the integrity of the hermit life and wield enormous social and political influence, something not achieved often in the history of the Church, East or West.

Sergius ushered in a golden age of Russian spiritual life, but although there was deep renewal, there were never any attempts to found new monastic orders. Russian monasticism still preserved the ancient traditions and to this day hermits continue to seek out remote places and people still seek them out in their 'desert'. This seems to be something of enormous vitality in Orthodoxy, which has survived the inroads of atheism; and St Sergius rightly remains one of the most popular of Russian saints.

St Seraphim of Sarov

The *staretz* (the 'elder') also remains a hidden yet vital element of Orthodox life, but it was in the nineteenth century particularly, on the eve of the virtual collapse of the Church, that the holy 'elders' came right to the fore and exerted an enormous influence on all strata of society. The monks at the monastery of Optina Pustyn (hermitage) have already been mentioned in chapter 6. Of the nineteenth-century Russian *startzy*, however, the first, and perhaps the best-known, is St Seraphim of Sarov.

Born at Kursk into family of provincial merchants, Seraphim was baptized with the name of Prokhor. When he was nineteen he entered a monastery in Sarov and took the name Seraphim. He spent the next fifteen years taking a full part in the life of the community, being ordained deacon first, and then priest, but becoming ever more aware of a call to solitude.

The spiritual tradition of St Symeon the New Theologian

In your light we see light. (Psalm 36:9)

Seraphim's first years of monastic life were during the period following the publication of the *Philokalia*, which had been translated into Russian in 1770, and it is thought that he may have been influenced by these spiritual writings. In order to get into Seraphim's life, it would be useful to flash back a few hundred years and take a brief look at the ascetic life of total self-renunciation and spiritual joy of a spiritual father known as St Symeon the New Theologian (AD949–1022). St Symeon's life followed the pattern of continual prayer, of bringing mind and heart in harmony, filled with the love of God. Despite his title, the 'New Theologian', Symeon was no narrow academic, but someone who taught of the riches of God from his own experience of prayer.

I move my foot and it is aglow with God.

Symeon's trust in God was so great and his renunciation of self-will was so total that he voluntarily went without food, trusting that God would prompt his senior to notice and invite him to eat. He 'did' urban theology for a quarter of a century as abbot of a busy community in the heart of the imperial capital, Constantinople; combining inner prayer with pastoral and administrative work. His prayer grew out of the scriptures, 'God be merciful to me a sinner' (Luke 18:13), but as he repeated the prayer of penitence he became flooded with joy and felt radiant light, uncreated, the living presence of God, fill the room so that he himself seemed turned into light. He was overwhelmed with tears of joy which marked his life and understanding of God for ever. Symeon felt himself wholly joined to God, but never at the cost of his own individuality. He wrote: 'Wretch though I be, I am the hand and foot of Christ. I move my hand and it is wholly Christ's hand. I move my foot and it is aglow with God.'

His vision of light affected his teaching and inspired hymns which are still included in anthologies of prayer.

You are higher than all essence, than the very nature of nature, higher than all ages, than all light... You are none of the things that are, but above them all.

You alone are God eternal, uncreated, O Holy Trinity, Father, Son and Spirit, creator of all that is seen and unseen! You are Lord and Master. You have wounded me with your love and transformed me. You have captured me with your beauty and I am transfixed, O Trinity, my

God! There are Three, and the features of Each are one, for the Three are One countenance, O my God, who are God of the whole universe! Let my eyes see your glory, for it is that which I announce in words every day, Creator and Master of all Ages, O Holy Trinity, my God!

Skarbnica Modlitw (Treasury of Prayer),
translation by Jenny Robertson

The all-important thing for St Symeon was to be united to God in continuing prayer, and it is exactly this tradition, passed on through Gregory Palamas and St Sergius of Radonezh, which Seraphim of Sarov lived out in his life as a monk. For him the aim of the Christian life was simply this: to abide in God and possess the Holy Spirit. 'Abide in me,' said Jesus to his disciples in the upper room, 'as I abide in you... Those who abide in me and I in you bear much fruit...' (John 15:4, 5). Seraphim took no part in political life; he wrote no treatises, led no new movement: he made it his life's work to abide in Christ and be filled with the Holy Spirit (Ephesians 5:18). And out of this life of silence, remoteness and prayer came lasting fruit.

---

*My soul waits for the Lord more than those who
watch for the morning.* (Psalm 130:6)

The icons show St Seraphim dressed in peasant homespun, his feet shod in shoes woven from birch bark. He is shown in the forest, kneeling on a stone in front of a tree on which is seen a simple icon of the mother of the Lord. This is, in fact, how Seraphim lived, for he withdrew from the monastery and led a life of seclusion in a hut he had made in the neighbouring forest. Here he lived in solitude for thirty years but, even so, people continually sought him out for help and counsel and he also continued to attend the church in the monastery. Seraphim lived a life of poverty and self-sufficiency. If he needed wood, he took an axe to a tree, he made his own shoes, collected berries, grew vegetables, studied the Bible and the Fathers—and prayed continually. In fact, at one period he spent a thousand nights without sleep, standing motionless on a small boulder in the total darkness of the forest giving the night watches to God. 'My soul waits for the Lord more than those who watch for the morning,' cries the psalmist (Psalm 130:6).

My sister has told me what those words used to mean to her when, a student nurse on night duty, she would see the first faint rays of dawn streak the sky beyond the hospital windows. She would have been glad, I think, if she had known someone was keeping watch. Seraphim did just that for three years on end, deep in the forests of Russia, where wild beasts prowled and robbers lurked.

I put my hope in your words. (Psalm 119:147)

Seraphim read the Bible as prayer, standing. He said at the end of his life, 'It's necessary to teach yourself to read [the scriptures] so that your understanding as it were swims in the Word of God, whose commands should direct your whole life. It is very useful to draw aside and read through the whole Bible intelligently—and God will not leave you without his kindness but will fill you with the gift of understanding.'

For all his hardness to himself, Seraphim was never hard on others. He preserved a gentle spirit through the years of solitude. Incredibly, he was once severely beaten up by robbers and suffered so badly that he had to return to the monastery for almost half a year, before he went back to his hut in the forest. However, even in seclusion he visited the monastery on Sundays and feast days, but his health failed, and when he could no longer walk he was given a small enclosed cell in the monastery. Here he continued his life of prayer. He now made it his habit to read through each of the four Gospels on each successive day from Monday to Thursday, a day for each Gospel. The monks would glance into his cell through the small barred window and see him standing, reading and praying together, for the Gospels had become his prayer. On the remaining two days of the week, Seraphim read the Acts and all the Epistles. And on Sunday he absorbed all the week's reading into the eucharist.

Thus, prayerfully standing and reading 'with his mind in his heart', Seraphim week by week accompanied the Lord through the annunciation, the birth in Bethlehem, the teaching and healing ministry by Galilee, Jerusalem and the upper room, Golgotha and the garden of the resurrection, and followed the story through the coming of the Spirit and the service of the apostles in the Church.

The kingdom of God is among you. (Luke 17:21)

At last, in 1825, he opened the door of his cell and people came from all over Russia, in their thousands, to see him. To many he brought healing; others he counselled, sometimes answering their questions before they had asked them. He also acted as spiritual director to the nuns of Diveevo, a neighbouring convent. The hallmark of all his conversations was gentleness undergirded with joy. He simply called people to Christ and poured out compassion and comfort to them. 'See,' he said joyfully, 'this kingdom of God is now found within us. The grace of the Holy Spirit shines forth and warms us, and, overflowing with many and varied scents into the air around us, regales our senses with heavenly delight, as it fills our hearts with joy inexpressible.'

A gentle, healing light...

One of the people who came to see Seraphim was a merchant called Nicholas Motovilov, who wrote down an account of their meetings. Two things in particular stand out: firstly Seraphim, like Symeon in the seventh century, and Gregory and Sergius in the fourteenth century—steeped as he was in 'the prayer of the heart', not least the Jesus Prayer—received visions of God as light, the sort of transfiguring experience which Symeon had recorded, linked with a great sense of joy and well-being. Secondly, Seraphim was so certain of the presence of Jesus and the infilling of the Holy Spirit that he could say with full assurance, 'The Holy Spirit fills with joy whatever he touches.'

Nicholas Motovilov and Seraphim had talked together about the work of the Holy Spirit as they walked through the forest. Seraphim said, 'We pray every day: "Holy Spirit, Comforter, Treasury of blessings and Giver of life, come and abide in us..." But he is with us all the time.'

'How can we know that he is with us and we are in him?' Motovilov wondered and, in answer, Seraphim stretched out his almost fleshless hands, took the merchant very firmly by the shoulders, and said, 'My son, we are both at this moment in the Spirit of God. Why don't you look at me?'

But Nicholas Motovilov turned away. Seraphim had become transfigured with light and it hurt his eyes to look.

Seraphim understood. 'Don't be afraid,' he said. Then bending his head closer towards Nicholas, he whispered very softly: 'Thank the Lord for his infinite goodness towards us... But why, my son, do you not look me in the eyes? Just look, and don't be afraid; the Lord is with us.'

Nicholas did as he was bidden and looked at Seraphim and felt himself filled with even greater awe. The light was real. It blinded him and spread around, making the snow which covered the forest sparkle blindingly. Snowflakes, which were steadily falling around them, became like myriad radiant splinters of diamond, each one a facet of light. It seemed as though Seraphim was speaking to him out of the very heart of the sun and Nicholas felt flooded through with an indescribable sense of well-being and peace. Seraphim explained gently that what they were both experiencing was 'the peace which passes all understanding', the very peace of which the Lord spoke when he said to his disciples: 'My peace I give to you; not as the world gives do I give to you.' 'What else do you feel?' Seraphim asked and Nicholas replied, 'Infinite joy in all my heart.'

And Seraphim said: 'When the Spirit of God comes down to a man and overshadows him with the fullness of his presence, then the man's soul overflows with unspeakable joy, for the Holy Spirit fills with joy whatever he touches...'

Wishful thinking? I first read those words when I was going through a very difficult time. Someone I loved dearly was terribly ill—a ghost, a shadow—and I had no warmth in my heart. Nothing was healed; I was wrung out with pain and pity, and yet I believed unshakeably that the gentleness, the light which transfigured flesh and snowbound forest was true, absolutely true...

And this light continued to shine in strange, mystical ways, beyond human explanation or accounting. In the terrible years after the revolution, prisoners were held in the forests of Sarov—and people tested beyond endurance felt that St Seraphim had left a healing presence in the forests and felt comforted beyond their pain. Furthermore, nuns from the convent of Diveevo who inherited the traditions Seraphim had sown when he served as spiritual director, were scattered into prison camps or swallowed up by enforced industrialization, but still continued a secret ministry as spiritual daughters of this gentle, Spirit-filled man.

I, too, felt the presence of St Seraphim once when a friend took me to a graveyard which bears the saint's name. It was winter: Russia was still officially atheist and although it was April, the earth was snowbound and the sky was grey, yet as we walked among the bare trees we felt that spring was beginning to stir in sap and birdsong. Above the gates of the graveyard was a sign whch proclaimed vaingloriously: Immortal Leningrad. Birches, eerily white against the grey sky, were crowded together as close as the gravestones—and as close as the housing blocks on the skyline beyond. But here, within the gates, on ground dedicated to St Seraphim, there was a tangible sense of well-being and peace.

We went into a small wooden church which bore Seraphim's name, and now the sense of peace was overwhelming. A few candles flickered in the darkness. A priest and a reader chanted prayers. One or two women gathered and bowed their foreheads to the wooden floor, then stood and silently absorbed the act of prayer, offering their needs, the hardship of their lives in an atheist state. A young couple walked slowly around the dimly lit church, just looking, not praying and yet they too, perhaps, were serving God in their own way. When we went away the wooden church which had seemed so dark and poor was now filled with the gentle light of many candle-flames.

CHAPTER 9

An Evangelist & Bible Teacher
FATHER ALEXANDER MEN
(1935—1990)

JEREMIAH 31:31—33

*I will make a new covenant with the house of Israel
and the house of Judah... I will put my law within them,
and I will write it on their hearts; and I will be their God
and they shall be my people.*

The way of the heart, the desert experience of hermit monks like
St Seraphim of Sarov, was continued in the nineteenth century by
a married man, a priest in a dockland parish, Father John of
Kronstadt (1829–1908). He was canonized in 1946 by the
Russian Orthodox Church in Exile. Father John lamented the fact
that, throughout the first years of his ministry, there was as yet no
Russian translation of the Bible. The only version was in Old
Church Slavonic, which made the scriptures unavailable to mil-
lions of Russian people. When the Russian Bible finally appeared
in 1876, Father John of Kronstadt actively encouraged the practice
of Bible reading.

*Are you so pure, perfect and holy without reading the Gospels that
you don't need to look at yourselves in this mirror? Or are you so terribly ugly spiritually that you're afraid of your ugly reflection? Approach
the scriptures and be enlightened so that 'your faces shall never be
ashamed' (Psalm 34:5).*

Father John practised what he preached. Speaking at a clergy gathering in a provincial town towards the end of his life he testified:

*Now I particularly love to read both Testaments, Old and New. I can-
not live without this reading. There is just so much contained within the*

holy pages, so many commands are opened up for the life of the human soul! So many people, striving for spiritual renewal, find all that is needful here for a complete rebirth. The holy scriptures are particularly essential for those of you who are preachers. There's an inexhaustible supply of themes for sermons here, only you must first learn how to edify yourself in order to teach others.

Truly I tell you, just as you did it one of the least of these who are members of my family, you did it to me. (Matthew 25:40)

Undergirding Father John's Spirit-filled and fruitful ministry was his belief that since the Son of God revealed himself as the Word of the Father, the words of scripture have the same power today as they had in the life of Christ. Father John was the Mother Teresa of Kronstadt. He met Christ quite literally in the poor, the beggars and the outcast and his ministry to them was simply his belief that Ephesians 1:18–23 means what it says: the Church is the Body of Christ endued with the same mighty power which raised the Lord from the tomb. Father John's ministry was based on continual prayer: whether he was visiting the poor and sick, teaching children, preaching or busy with charitable work, he prayed and he encouraged others to do the same. He has left a small book, called *My Life in Christ*, which he wrote for his spiritual children. In it he describes how he prayed before the liturgy, prayed at every moment during its celebration, prayed on his way home, a conscious effort of will and heart. It is, after all, so easy, not to pray!

Your Name is Love...

Lord, Your Name is Love,
do not reject me, lost and astray.
Your Name is Power—
strengthen me, feeble and falling.
Your Name is Light,
flood my suffering soul.

Your Name is Peace,
calm my troubled heart.
Your Name is Mercy—
never cease from showing mercy to me and mine.

Father John of Kronstadt, trans. Jenny Robertson

Like St Seraphim, Father John had healing powers and the gift of spiritual counsel and discernment. People pressed about him wherever he went, longing to draw power and help from him. Once, in a vast crowd he singled out a Jewish woman—and healed her of the migraines which made her life a misery. Through that one action grace spread, all unknown, through her family until it flowered in the life of a great evangelist and Bible teacher, Father Alexander Men.

The measure of Father Alexander's importance is, horrifyingly, his murder and the total silence which has followed it, together with the way his books have now disappeared from Orthodox shops. It is a tired axiom that in the Soviet era in which the newspapers *Pravda* (*Truth*) told lies and *Izvestia* (*News*) contained no news, you had to learn to read between the lines. And the sub-text here is that the weapon which hacked Father Men to death—an axe—has been traditionally the way the Jews were murdered.

However, all that was far in the future, the day in Kronstadt when a Jewish woman felt her headache disappear. She never found faith in Christ, but her daughter Elena, Alexander Men's mother, born two years after Father John's death, was drawn towards the Christian faith. She was encouraged in her difficult path by her elder cousin, Vera, with whom she lived for a while.

This was in the 1930s, when anti-religious propaganda was enforced upon people, when atheists 'celebrated' major church festivals by parading through the streets carrying banners with crude, often blasphemous, slogans. Yet an onlooker at one of these parades reports that the crude caricatures produced no laughter, the bright red banners no joy. People had been terrorized into silence and could not protest, but neither did they applaud; they did their best to get out of the way as the processions wound their way through the city streets.

Alexander Men's aunt, Vera, has left an account of her own path to faith. It was published after Father Men's death in a collection of writings called *I bylo utro* ('And it was morning'). It is a remarkable piece of spiritual writing, coming, as it does, from the period of most virulent attacks on all forms of belief. Niece of the Jewish woman healed in Kronstadt, cousin of Elena Men, Vera was born into a middle-class Jewish family which was not particularly religious. On holiday at the family country house, the fourteen-year-old girl watched the peasants observe church festivals in the traditional way, watched the pageantry and processions, but also the devotion, and felt drawn towards this with the age-old tug at the heartstrings experienced by an ethnic minority: Is this not my tradition too? Am I not Russian? I speak the language of this people, yet their ways are not my ways... Then came the revolution and she had enough to think about, studying—she trained as a child psychologist—and simply struggling to survive. Atheism took an ever greater hold. In 1927 Metropolitan Sergei, who was acting in the name of the Patriarch, made a statement of loyalty to the Soviet State, compromising the church and giving the totalitarian government an easy route into control of every aspect of church life. His slavish stance simply unleashed persecution on the church: bishops and priests were arrested, church buildings were turned into museums of atheism, into public baths, underground stations, warehouses... or simply left to rot; icons and church furnishings were hacked to pieces, and what was left of the church in the truest sense of the word simply went underground. Twenty-three years later, when Laurens van der Post visited the closed, controlled world of the Soviet Union, he recorded that he found a sense of conformity so total that some of his tour group couldn't stand it and went home—and that all signs of religious life were conspicuous only by their total absence.

Even whispers are dangerous...

In the 1930s, people didn't dare even whisper to one another about God. I had a little hint of what it must have meant to live under terror just the other day in the heart of Warsaw, now a free city in a democratic country. An elderly man, slightly built and straight as a ramrod, whose humanity and capacity for survival shone in his blue eyes, was talking to us about the Second World War: he had served in the Polish Home Army—whose heroism is only now being officially recognized in Poland—and had been sent to Siberia for three years. All these years later he lowered his voice and glanced over his shoulder as he talked—a gesture more telling than words.

Thus it was that one day, standing at a compulsory gathering in praise of the Soviet State (non-attendance was always noted—and punished), Vera saw that the young woman close beside her remained silent during the singing of an atheistic hymn. She took careful note, for she too had been unable to sing these words. Somehow they managed to get into conversation as the crowds left the square and it turned out that they were colleagues at work. Little by little, Vera learned more about the Christian faith from this young woman, Olga, who took her secretly out to the town of Zagorsk (the place where St Sergius of Radonezh had founded his Holy Trinity monastery). Here, in a small wooden house on the edge of the town, cared for by two secret nuns from the convent of Diveevo where St Seraphim of Sarov had once given spiritual direction and counsel, was a 'catacomb' priest whose name in religion was also Seraphim.

Father Seraphim, priested at the age of thirty-nine in 1919, had simply gone underground rather than serve in the compromised official church. His spiritual children from two different Moscow parishes came secretly to pray, confess, have their children baptized or simply to visit their priest.

Soon Vera became one of Father Seraphim's clandestine flock and, whenever she could, she travelled out of town to visit him, never telling anyone at home where she was going. In 1935 she took her younger cousin, Elena, now married and with a baby son of nine months, Alexander. Father Seraphim baptized Elena and her baby. Soon afterwards Vera herself accepted baptism and thereafter she dedicated her life to caring for her cousin and her children.

In 1941 the German army invaded the Soviet Union. Elena was urged by her husband to leave Moscow with the boys and join him in Ekaterinburg, but Father Seraphim counselled differently. He advised Elena to move out to Zagorsk with Alexander and his baby brother, promising her that they would be kept safe there under the protection of St Sergius. Elena did so and Vera frequently joined her cousin, bringing food and supplies as best she could, making the journey by trains which were often delayed for hours on end—but she always found a way through her difficulties and discovered she was protected in every danger.

A year later Father Seraphim died, but not before he had heard seven-year-old Alexander's first confession and predicted that he would become a man of great influence in Russia.

Having nothing, yet possessing everything. (2 Corinthians 6:10)

Thus, in atheistic Russia, Alexander grew up in a Christian family—but with his roots in Judaism and his spiritual nurture in the hands of secret nuns who carried on the great Russian tradition of the wilderness in the city and the prayer of the heart. Their lives embodied the life of the Spirit, with joy as the hallmark. He lived in a single room in a communal flat with his parents, his Aunt Vera and his younger brother. It is very hard—indeed, inhuman—to live and eat and sleep and study in one room, children and adults together, to share a cooker and sink and toilet with far too many other people who may be drunk or abusive, untidy or obsessive about tidiness, who would certainly have been anti-Semitic, but against this background and with all the rigidity and narrowness of the Soviet school, Alexander became fluent in at least one other language, French, and read widely: even books by forbidden writers seemed to find their way to him. By his early teens he was reading Kant and the great Russian religious philosophers. From his grandparents he absorbed a knowledge of Judaism, of the festivals and fasts which formed the background of the life of Jesus, providing links between the two which were obvious, joyful and clear and which form such an important part of his first published book, *Son of Man*.

Being Russian, young Alexander learned off by heart volumes of poetry—but he did not confine his reading to the writers who were permitted and almost deified by the Soviets, but also read the much-maligned Dostoyevsky, the Church Fathers, books on Western Christianity and, of course, the Bible, which he would later expound with such clarity and life that his words leap off the page. Encouraged by the nuns who continued to lead their secret life of prayer, Alexander also read biblical criticism and by the time he was eighteen he was actually following the study course of the seminary on his own.

You hem me in, behind and before,
and lay your hand upon me. (Psalm 139:5)

With the incriminating word 'Jew' stamped on his personal documents, Alexander was denied access to the university. He continued to read theology and philosophy—but was formally enrolled in the Institute of Forestry and Fur in Moscow, which allowed him to study another favourite subject, biology. During his course the Institute transferred to Siberia and here unfolded another of the coincidences which are really the workings of grace, for Alexander met another future priest, Gleb Yakunin—and indeed, this meeting was a turning-point in the life of the younger man, for it came at a time when he was questioning the faith he had received from his mother in early childhood. Father Gleb Yakunin would later become known in the West when a stringent prison sentence sent him to a labour camp for six years to Yakutia in north-east Siberia, where the temperature drops below sixty degrees for months on end.

In 1956 Alexander married. He was twenty-one. His bride, Natalya, was a fellow student. In those years immediately following Stalin's death there was an official 'thaw': the nation which had wept at the death of their kind, good leader who had given them all a wonderful life in the best nation in the world, now heard, shocked, of his crimes; prisoners were released from the camps, some sort of rehabilitation began. But nothing eased up for the churches. Krushchev unleashed a bitter attack on all denominations. Clergy and lay-people were subjected to psychiatric abuse, monasteries and Baptist prayer houses alike were closed and children of believing parents were abused too, held up to ridicule in the classroom, or, in some cases actually sent away from home to be brought up in State orphanages, where they suffered physical as well as spiritual and emotional neglect.

This wave of harsh measures affected Alexander. The authorities, knowing of his active links with the cathedral in Irkutsk, refused to let him sit his final exams. He was sent back to Moscow with his wife and baby daughter, but there, without attending seminary, which would have been closed to him in any case, he was ordained deacon and, in 1960, priest.

The young priest was not allowed to serve in Moscow. He was sent out to the sticks and life must have been very hard for Natalya, coping with domestic life in a small village with absolutely no amenities, while her husband was immersed in parish life, in studying and writing. His output was prodigious, his erudition outstanding, but he never ceased to be a 'people' person and someone who knew him in those early years of his ministry noted how he had the ability to put everyone at his ease, from the peasant women of his parish to the blasé and spiritually starved Moscow intelligentsia—and even disarmed the factotums of lower Soviet officialdom both in and out of the church.

We are ambassadors for Christ, since God is making his appeal through us, we entreat you on behalf of Christ, be reconciled to God. (2 Corinthians 5:20)

This ease with people, together with his tremendous learning in so many fields besides theology—Eastern and Western philosophy, nature and biology, Russian and European literature—as well as his devotion to Christ and ultimately simple faith, sparkled from every talk he gave and every page he wrote. This is what makes his books so readable. Father Alexander was a true 'ambassador for Christ' to his own people within their closed country.

Indeed, he drew people to him like a magnet. Like Anatoly Levitin, who admired him immensely, Father Alexander held open home on a fixed day each week during the later years of the 1960s and the suburban trains would bring his visitors out of Moscow. They were friends and most were believers, so they would travel together; the latest piece of *samizdat* (self-published and highly dangerous literature) would be passed from hand to hand. Those who had read it would discuss it eagerly; those who had not would borrow it and spend the entire two-hour train journey huddled on a wooden seat, or standing strap-hanging, avidly reading forbidden literature. Poets and artists, song-writers and professors, students and philosophers would all be part of the gatherings and Father Alexander would meet them in the small wooden porch outside his house, pray with them and they would crowd into his study for the evening. Some people headed straight for his library, which boasted one of the largest collections of religious and philosophical books in private hands. They would pore over volumes unobtainable elsewhere, borrow them and the books would circulate around Moscow, passing from reader to reader, sometimes taking a year or more to return to their owner.

The KGB knew about the library, but somehow never attacked it. It was a unique resource of spiritual writing, and people said of Father Alexander that he was 'a missionary sent by God to the wild tribe of the Soviet intelligentsia'.

People felt affirmed by Father Alexander. Believing parents who struggled because they were too afraid not to send their children to the Communist youth organizations were encouraged to learn that Father Alexander's children were Pioneers too. But for these —and other parents—Father Alexander wrote an illustrated book explaining God to children who, from their earliest years, were taught in an educational system which deified Lenin and denied God. He and his friends translated Western spiritual literature into Russian, making writers like Teilhard du Chardin available, while he also continued his own studies, graduating from Moscow Theological Academy with a degree in religion in Ancient Babylon.

Dissidents like Gleb Yakunin continued to be close friends of Father Men, but he was never drawn to participate in politics. His desire, following the age-old traditions of Orthodoxy, was to convert the heart. After Soviet tanks invaded Czechoslovakia in 1968, Father Alexander stopped holding 'open days' in the same way.

Behind locked doors...

The vision and prayerful atmosphere of the open days continued back in Moscow. Friends would gather in someone's room, pray together and read the Gospels. Some of them took to meeting together on Sundays. Like the disciples of old, they met behind locked doors (John 20:19), with curtains closed. At every knock on the door, they would look round, afraid, and quickly slip the precious New Testament into a hiding-place—for someone might have been followed, and this new knock could herald the agents of the secret police, and the Bibles they confiscated could not be replaced (from 'Father Alexander Men', Alexander Dubrov, *RCL*, Vol 2, Nos 3–4, October 1974).

But at this time of repression a chance meeting with a French-woman of Russian origins opened a doorway for Alexander Men. He spoke of his concern about the dearth of spiritual literature in Russia, of the growing numbers of people who had newly come to faith, or were seeking for meaning in the unfreedom of the Brezhnev years. She put him in touch with French publishers, 'La Vie avec Dieu', and so began a long and fruitful partnership which lasted right up until *glasnost*.

Considering the stringent controls at Soviet customs, it is amazing that Father Alexander's manuscripts were able to be taken out of the country—and the published works brought back in. It is also amazing how a busy parish priest charged with the cure of souls of simple peasants and the Moscow intelligentsia alike, the round of lengthy services, with baptisms, weddings, funerals in addition, the hearing of confessions and the work of spiritual direction, could write so much, read so deeply, not least in a country where the activities of daily living, no matter how trivial, involve inordinate amounts of time, know-how, contacts, paperwork, patience. How much more the running of a parish and the feeding of a family of teenage children!

Novaya Derevnya, 1970–1990

In 1970, Father Alexander was moved to a new parish, Novaya Derevnya, closer to Moscow, situated on the old road which ran from Moscow to the town still known as Zagorsk. This simple wooden church now became a mecca for people from Moscow who rented holiday homes in the area each summer. The small groups for prayer and Bible study—and simple human friendship in a city of eight million—continued and spread until a network was formed, a distinctive part of Father Alexander's ministry.

Of course the KGB took note. Father Alexander was constantly watched and harried—but it's likely he had built up a good relationship with the stooges who were set to watch him and word would be passed around that it was better not to make the journey out of Moscow for a bit, or even to stop the group meetings for a while.

The early 1980s saw the regime turn vicious: ex-chief of the KGB, Yuri Andropov, was elected to follow Brezhnev and because he was virtually moribund, the powers that be in the Kremlin determined to show their strength: there were new repressions, new arrests, and Father Alexander was called in for almost daily questioning. The breakthrough came only in 1986, with high-level talks in Iceland between Presidents Reagan and Gorbachev. Prominent prisoners were freed—these included Vladimir Poresh, Irina Ratushinskaya, Father Gleb Yakunin, and Sakharov. The showdown came in 1988, with the celebrations to commemorate the Thousand Years of the Baptism of Russia. Father Men's books started to be published in Russia; foreigners of every Christian denomination began to seek him out. He now worked openly, starting a Sunday School in his own parish, lecturing on basic Christian truths, on the dogmas of the Church, on comparative religion, on the creeds—to capacity audiences. In the early years these lectures would be interrupted by the noise of motor-bikes revving up, or the playing of loud music. He treated these with the humour which was typical of him, so that they actually pointed up the truth of what he was saying.

The hidden homeland of the spirit...

As things became freer, his life became even more frenetic. In 1990 he baptized sixty adults; he took part in the opening of the Bible Society in Russia, founded a new university, a cultural association. On 1 September 1990 Father Alexander celebrated the thirtieth anniversary of his ordination. On 8 September he gave an outstanding lecture, *To be a Christian*. Here are a few extracts from Father Men's talk:

Human beings have two countries, two homelands. One is our own country, that place where each of us was born and grew up. But the other is the hidden homeland of the spirit which the eye may not see and the ear may not hear but where, by our nature, we belong. We are children of the earth and at the same time visitors to it...

In the religion of the Old Testament... there developed the notion of faith as trust... the moment when a person says to God, 'Yes, I accept, I am listening.' So the ancient covenant between God and humanity was born, the ancient alliance... In the seventh century before our era the prophet Jeremiah said, 'Thus says the Lord, I will make with my people a New Covenant (Hebrew berit ha-das—a new testament, a new alliance), not like the old one, the former one. I will write it on their hearts' [Jeremiah 31:31–33 paraphrased]. And then one night the sacrifice was celebrated. Seven hundred years after the prophet Jeremiah, in a small room, twelve men gathered together for the sacrifice. Usually the sacrifice was made with blood, for blood is the symbol of life, and life belongs to God alone... That night I was speaking of, in the spring of the thirtieth year of the first century of our era, Jesus of Nazareth, surrounded by the Twelve, celebrated the ritual—the memorial of the freedom which God bestows. There was no blood, but a chalice of wine and bread, and he broke this bread and gave it to them all and said, 'This is my body.' And he passed the chalice round the disciples and said, 'This is my blood, which is shed for you; this is the new covenant of my blood.'

And so, at this holy table, God and humanity were joined together... Christianity is not a new ethical system, but a new life whch leads us into direct contact with God. It is a new alliance, a New Testament... Christ reveals God to us as our heavenly Father, and by this revelation we are made brothers and sisters to one another, for brothers and sisters are those who have a common father.

And now we know that our common spiritual Father is God, and our hearts are opened to the good news of Jesus; that is the mystery of the Gospels.

Anyone of you knows perfectly well how confused people are, how weak, how many complications and sins have taken root in us. But there is a power which Christ left on earth, which is given to us for free: it is called grace. In Russian the word is blagodat—'the good' (blago) which is 'given' (dat) for free. You don't have to work for it; it's a gift...

I am talking about the very essence of the Christian faith...

Christianity is the sanctification of the world, the victory over evil, over darkness, over sin. But it is the victory of God. It began on the night of the resurrection, and it will continue as long as the world exists.

Christianity for the Twenty-First Century: The Life and Work of
Alexander Men, *Elizabeth Roberts and Ann Shukman, 1996*

Father Alexander ended his lecture. As usual he allowed time for questions from the floor. He talked until late in the evening, gathered his things together, made his way to the train station, travelled out of town, walked through the woods with the yellowing leaves of early September, his mind was racing, as usual after these lectures. He still had so much to do, so much to formulate. Night was always too brief.

On his way to church next morning, he was struck down with an axe. Not realizing at first how serious the wound was, he continued on his way to the station, but there he felt faint and knew he wouldn't make it to church that day. He turned back through the woods, but it was a long way home. Father Alexander reached the gate of his wooden house in the forest but got no further. He collapsed and died.

His last public words, then, had been an affirmation of the victory of God which spoke right to the heart of his audience. Western apologetics were just about to flood the Russian market. Preachers and Bible teachers were already starting to bring their latest books and commentaries, newly translated. Evangelists put up huge banners promising healings and wonders. None of these spoke to the Russian people as Father Men could. 'We make the journey together,' he truly said. He understood the mindset of someone brought up in a closed society; to people in a culture which enforced love of the homeland, which made—and still makes—a distinction between citizens and visitors, he said, 'We are children of the earth and at the same time visitors to it...'

A true missionary in the Soviet wilderness

When I was living and working in Russia, teaching the Bible to children, talking about the faith to friends, I devoured Father Alexander's books. I think anyone who loves the Bible would, but the important thing was that he spoke from the heart of the culture to his own people, a true missionary in the Soviet wilderness. He knew the gaps in their spiritual knowledge; he knew how to fill them; he knew where those who explored yoga and Eastern philosophies were coming from, where those who loved literature and culture might find the best links into faith. He wrote beautiful Russian prose—and the bibliographies in his books are wide-ranging, quoting authors from all the main European thought-streams, as well as Russians. His lectures on the Gospels, on the apostle Paul, were a mainstay for me when I was teaching more senior pupils. I fell on his books wherever I saw them—and at first that might be in a kiosk in the theatre, at a street corner, in church. I bought them over again and gave them away to friends, particularly Jewish friends, for Father Alexander affirms Judaism in a culture whose anti-Semitism was almost certainly one of the causes of his death.

One of his books, *Son of Man*, I turn to again and again. He began it when he was still in his teens, living with his family in that single room in their Moscow flat. It was one of the first books he published abroad, under a pseudonym; it simply retells the Gospels, reading almost like a novel in lyrical prose, setting the story in its historical context, explaining the Roman and Greek background as well as very beautifully giving its Jewish setting. An edition of this book was printed by a Protestant publisher and given out at a Billy Graham crusade, along with New Testaments and other literature for enquirers and I noticed an immediate change. *Son of Man* disappeared for a while and when it reappeared it was no longer in Orthodox sections in Christian bookshops. However, the cultural association and the university Father Alexander helped to found still continues in his name, though in the present hardening up of the Orthodox leadership I'm sure they are experiencing difficulties. His followers are many, from all walks of life and from many nations of the world, and his works are still being reprinted, but my experience in St Petersburg, at any rate, is that they are no longer easy to find.

I only know Father Alexander Men through his books, but he speaks so directly to his reader that I feel I know his voice. However, my husband once was privileged to have a face-to-face encounter, in Moscow in June 1990. He had heard there was to be a series of lectures on the Bible and he went along. Lecture after lecture was given—totally boring and dull. One of the many paradoxes of Russian life is that this nation of singers, who make the reading of poetry come alive, become boring mutterers when it comes to giving a lecture, rambling away without notes, a self-indulgent ego-trip it often seems to me. I could only put it down to years of being forced to listen to diatribes on topics no one wanted to hear, while the things they did had to be whispered anyway!

But then a priest, handsome, with greying hair and beard, came forward—and the whole meeting took off. His talk was riveting, full of knowledge, making the Bible utterly relevant. 'Who is that man?' my husband asked a friend. 'Oh, don't you know?' came the reply. 'That's Father Alexander Men.'

Father Alexander was always open to Christians from other denominations. He opened up new possibilities of dialogue. In Father Men the Russian Orthodox Church had one of its ablest advocates. His murder, and the pointed silence which followed it, only confirm the deep-seated xenophobia and blinkered narrowness of an orthodoxy which continues to silence its prophets (Matthew 23:37). For Father Men, that morning of 9 September, daylight had dawned, but for the Church he leaves behind, there is now an impression of ambiguity where there had been a real hope of openness and light.

CHAPTER 10

THE BIBLE IN RUSSIA

The ordinances of the Lord are true and righteous altogether.
More to be desired are they than gold, even much fine gold;
sweeter also than honey, and drippings of the honeycomb.

———

There is a book whose every word is commentated on, explained
and preached in all the ends of the earth, applied to every
possible circumstance of life. This book is the Gospel—and its
charm is infinitely fresh, so that when, satiated with the world or
burdened with sorrow, we chance to open it, we find ourselves
unable to resist being carried away by its sweetness and we
immerse ourselves spiritually in divine oratory.

So wrote the greatest of Russian poets, Alexander Pushkin (1799–1837), who is to Russian literature what Shakespeare is to English, and to Russian poetry what Burns is to Scottish, while Dostoevsky exclaimed: 'What a wonderful book is Holy Scripture, what a miracle and what strength this book gives to humankind! What an exact representation of the world, of people and of human characteristics! Here everything is named and shown, world without end! And how many mysteries are solved, how much is revealed!'

Although until the Soviet era a large proportion of Russia remained illiterate, people were not totally unschooled biblically. My husband has worked in St Petersburg with a group of Slavists who were compiling a dictionary of Bible sayings in the Russian language. They examined proverbs and quotations from all sources of literature to see which of them were biblical, and while many Bible sayings had come into common use in the eighteenth and nineteenth centuries, others had found their way into the language in the older Slavonic form, showing that the Bible had played an important part in the language of the people from quite early on.

The Communists took Bible texts and twisted them for their own ends: 'Who is not with us is against us.' 'He who takes the sword will die by the sword'—this last, blazoned on red banners to propagate world peace, was quoted in Eisenstein's influential film, *Alexander Nevsky*, and most people attribute the saying to the thirteenth-century hero. Perhaps the rawest mockery of all was the homage paid to Lenin with the words: 'Lenin lived, Lenin lives and Lenin will live', an unpleasant distortion of Christian truth in general and Hebrews 13:8 in particular.

The Bible in Russia—early years

The first Slavonic translations of holy scripture, which had been made by the missionary saints Cyril and Methodius in the ninth century, began to appear in Kievan Rus in the tenth century. They appeared as separate books—the first complete Bible to appear in Russia as one whole book did so only towards the end of the fifteenth century. From the fire and plunder of medieval Russia some five thousand examples of manuscripts with the names of Old Testament books have survived, and double that number of New Testament lists. These were mainly in the form of extracts of scripture to be used for reading during the services, from the Acts, Epistles and Gospels. It is generally thought that the typical picture in Old Russia was that people heard the scriptures during the church services, rather than read them for themselves. It is useful to recall that the whole structure of the Church was designed to embody truths of scripture and the icons which surrounded the humblest peasant were an illustrated Bible against the background of which a woman or man, however uneducated, could understand visually the words they heard in church.

Orthodoxy has always understood scripture in the light of tradition. The thought here is that the canon of scripture was chosen by the Church, and so it is the Church which must be allowed to be the interpreter of scripture, rather than the individual. The text cited is Acts 8:30–31: when Philip asks the Ethiopian eunuch if he understands what he is reading, the reply comes: 'How can I unless someone explains it to me?'

The Bible came into Russia from Byzantium accompanied by

manuscripts with the relevant commentaries. Many of the princes of Kievan Rus, both secular and ecclesiastical, were highly educated in the schools of Byzantium and Athos, as indeed were many monks who undertook Bible study in obedience to their spiritual father. Asceticism, prayer, sacrament, deeds of mercy and the reading of the scriptures were seen as one, and all were emphasized as essential spiritual exercises.

'I beg you to read the holy books diligently'

The great spiritual leaders of Russia in every century have valued the Bible and urged people to read it. 'Therefore I beg you to read the holy books diligently,' urged St Cyril of Turov in the twelfth century, 'so that feeding on the Word of God you may reach the untold blessedness of eternal life.'

In his sermons, Cyril treated the reading of the Word as the privilege of many, not the duty of an isolated few. The Christian, he said, 'is someone who has found the treasury of holy books, the prophets, the Psalter, the Acts and Epistles and also the very speech of the Saviour himself, Jesus Christ, and reflecting on this with a true mind finds salvation not only for himself, but also for many others who pay attention to him.'

Nil Sorski (1433–1508) and the Non-Possessors

I put aside the thing I have to do, and read the scriptures first.

St Cyril was not alone in speaking of the fruit of immersing the mind in the Word of God, but one of the great Christian figures of medieval Russia, Nil Sorski (1433–1508), was the first to point out that holy scripture not only defines the basic principles of the Christian life but actually directs us in all our actions. Nil, or Nilus, was a hermit monk living in a remote area beyond the Volga. He led a movement known as the Non-Possessors, attacking not only the ownership of property by monks, but also the way the monastic overlords treated the peasants whose land they claimed. Nil spoke out against the way the Church used the arm of the State to coerce compliance from heretics—a departure which St Sergius of Radonezh would surely also have deplored. Sergius had been able to act powerfully in the political life of the time, whilst retaining his spiritual, other-worldly life of prayer and fasting. After his day the Church lost that clear distinction and Nil argued forcibly for a simplicity of life based on prayer and the study of scripture: 'I dare not undertake any task without first soaking myself in the Word of God,' he wrote. 'And if I haven't yet done so, I put aside the thing I have to do, and read the scriptures first. When I turn to the grace of God, then the things I do are filled with blessedness.'

Nil guided his novices and pupils by classifying the texts used in the church services so that they might see how the readings fitted together: the commands of the Lord Jesus came first, then the writings of the apostles and after that the works of the Fathers, and the basis of it all were the words which end the Sermon on the Mount in Matthew's Gospel: 'Everyone then who hears these words of mine and puts them into practice is like a wise man who built his house on rock' (Matthew 7:24, NIV).

Although Nil was canonized by the Church, the Non-Possessors lost out to those who wanted the Church and State to be more closely linked, not least in the imposition of religious conformity. However, towards the end of the fifteenth century, a major event in the history of the Bible in Russia took place in Novgorod when, in response to a breakaway movement which taught that the prophecies of the Old Testament were not yet fulfilled, the Messiah had not yet come, a complete codex of the Slavonic Bible books was established, which included textual editing of the original Byzantine manuscripts.

Maximus the Greek (c. 1470–1556)

In the wake of this, a scholar-monk from Athos, Maximus the Greek, was invited to Russia. Although he had been born in Greece he had lived in Florence and Venice, where he had espoused many of the ideas of the Renaissance, turned from them under the influence of the fiery reformer, Savronola. He actually became a

Dominican, but found his spiritual search fulfilled in the monastery on Mount Athos, where he truly tried to carry out the command of Christ and make himself 'the slave of all' (Mark 10:45). Maximus came to Russia at the invitation of the Tsar, with the specific task of translating into Russian Greek Bible commentaries which were not yet known in Russia and of checking errors in liturgical books. Maximus also translated the Psalter and the Russian Church is indebted to him for opening up a new level in the understanding of scripture. Unfortunately for the Church, however, Maximus was viewed with distrust. He was attacked by the authorities both for the changes he tried to make in the liturgies and because, believing that the path of discipleship means self-denial, self-stripping and walking the way of the cross (Mark 8:34), he flung his lot in with the Non-Possessors. As a result, far from using the great gifts of a scholarly, widely travelled and deeply spiritual man, the Church of the day had him imprisoned for twenty-six years.

First printed Slavonic Bible, 1580

Russia was by now reeling under the cruelties of Ivan the Terrible, who had begun his reign as a deeply pious young man, but became increasingly plunged into dark depressions and paranoia. Bible learning suffered a severe setback. None the less, in 1580 the first printed version of the Slavonic Bible was made in south-west Russia. Printing presses were speedily set up in Moscow and the Gospels, Epistles and Psalter were soon coming off the presses. 1663 saw the appearance in Moscow of the whole Slavonic Bible. These books were circulated widely, but rarely in the homes of the laity. However, a system of libraries was set up in the seventeenth century and the Bible was available there; moreover, by now many parish churches had their own printed copy of the Bible, which people could make use of for their own private reading. The Bible was also used in parish schools and before long clergy were urging lay people to make the daily reading of scripture part of their life of prayer.

> *Go therefore and make disciples of all nations… teaching them to obey everything that I have commanded you.* (Matthew 28:19–20)

The Bible had long been used by missionaries. In the dark days of restriction and contraction under the lordship of Tartar khans, the Christian faith united the Russian people and saved them from despair. They sent missionaries out among their conquerors—for though they paid tribute to the Tartars, under whose yoke they lived in bondage, they offered them in return the yoke of Christ. As early as 1261, Mitrophan went as a missionary bishop to Sarai, the Tartar capital on the Volga. Others preached, not among the Mongols, but among pagan tribes in the north-east and far north and, like Cyril and Methodius, these missionary-monks translated the Bible and church services into the languages and dialects of the people. Stephen, Bishop of Perm (1340–96) is an example of one of these early Bible translators. He spent thirteen years of preparation in a monastery, studying not only native dialects of the Finnic people he intended to serve, but also Greek in order to be better fitted for the work of Bible translation. Cyril and Methodius had adapted the Greek alphabet, but Stephen made use of native runes to systemize the Zyrian language and reduce it to writing. Born at Ustiug, north-east of Vologda, in the area of his future ministry, he had been open from boyhood to the language and culture of the Zyrian people, his future converts. He was also an icon painter and used these gifts to teach visually the truths of the scriptures he translated. A true scholar, his work not only bears the marks of great devotion but also was highly efficient and systematic. He went all through the Perm region (where, six hundred years later, other priests and Christian believers of all denominations would follow, for this area was widely networked by Soviet prison camps). In his day, however, Stephen dealt with heathen magicians and destroyed their idols. He taught young men to read and write and trained them to be teachers and clergy, laying the foundations of a native church. In 1383 he was made bishop and his sphere of activity increased. Not content with being a linguist, Bible translator and Christian teacher, Stephen was a true pastor: generous and open-handed within his diocese, he was a worker for justice and human rights and championed his people against attack and oppression in Novgorod and Moscow.

'Following him we will not stray'

Against secularization introduced by Peter the Great's reforms in the eighteenth century, church leaders still urged people to turn to scripture. St Tikhon of Zadonsk (1724–83), said:

Such a skilful and wise leader is shown us in the Gospel, Christ the son of God, of whom the Father says to us from heaven: 'This is my Son, the Beloved; in him I am well pleased; listen to him' (Matthew 17:5). That is, I sent him to you as a teacher, mentor and guide. When you want to come to me and receive the kingdom of heaven which you have lost, listen to what he has to teach. But the Lord says about himself: 'I am the way, the truth, and the life. No one comes to the Father except through me' (John 14:6). If then, dear Christians, we do not wish to stray finally and be for ever the prisoners of the devil, but rather wish to come to God and receive eternal life, to which we are called and born again through the waters of baptism, then we must entrust ourselves irreversibly to him, hold to him by faith and love, listen to his holy and true teaching, follow his footsteps, imitate the pure example of his sinless life... Following him we will not stray from the right path, but will come to the desired fatherland and house of our Heavenly Father where 'there are many dwelling places' (John 14:2). This way is a humble and lowly one, beloved Christians, but it leads those who take it to high heaven.

On True Christianity, 1771, quoted RCL Vol 1, No 1, 1973

Tikhon taught in the seminary in Tver, in the region of Moscow and served as Bishop of Voronezh in the south. His life was steeped in prayer and in the scriptures; in fact, the two were closely interwoven, as we see in the following prayers:

O, most blessed and merciful Jesus, our gracious Saviour! Do not leave us sinners, whom you redeemed with your holy blood; but knock, knock, on the door of our stone hearts, knock firmly with your saving and most sweet voice, and we will awake from our deep sinful sleep and will hear your most sweet and kind voice, for your voice is sweet and your form is beautiful, and thus will we ourselves begin to ask, seek and knock, knock on the door of your mercy (Song of Solomon 5:10, 16; Matthew 7:7–8).

Jesus, Son of God, Saviour who renews the world, renew me with the grace of your life-giving Spirit! Give me a mind to understand the power of your saving Advent; give me a heart to love You—the eternal love, comfort and joy of the saints; give me eyes to gaze unceasingly upon your Passion, give me ears to hear your holy word; give me lips to speak worthily to you, and in a way which is beneficial to me and my neighbour; give me feet to follow the way of your commandments; and, I pray, take all that is mine and give me what is yours; take what is worn out and give me all that is new, for you have created all things and without you we can do nothing, for you are blessed for ever.

On True Christianity, *quoted* RCL

St Tikhon was a fluent and engaging preacher. We can sense something of the love which welled from his lips as we follow these extracts from his writings, prayers and sermons. He had a personal love of the Lord and a total commitment to his Word:

Holy Scripture has been given to me and you, O man, as well as to all humankind by God. Every time we read the Scripture ourselves or have them read to us by the servants of God we converse with God. The Word of God is a heavenly gift and we should prepare ourselves carefully before we read it. As we approach Holy Writ we should resolutely lay aside everything which doesn't correspond to God's gift. Our reading should anticipate prayer, and prayer should anticipate the cleansing of our mind.

Although holy scripture has been given to all, St Tikhon stressed that only the truly repentant may receive the gospel.

Who then is deemed worthy of the gospel? The answer is: sinners who have turned from their sins to God, who, sick with sin, fearing the judgment of God, sorrowing and broken-hearted, seek the mercy of God and humbly fall down before him... The scriptures are no use without repentance. The gospel brings great consolation, but what can that consolation mean to someone who does not possess a sorrowful and broken heart? So you see we really need to know the Old Testament Law of God as well as his holy gospel and study both in depth, for the Law teaches us to recognize our sinfulness and to repent with a broken heart, while from the holy gospel we draw life-giving and true consolation. The Law given by Moses awakens the conscience of the sinner, it teaches you what you, Christian, should do; it exposes your faults, but to the broken-hearted God has already prepared news of salvation. The gospel does not leave you in despair; it supports the fallen and strengthens the feeble. The gospels are the true hope of the hopeless. Simply receive the will of God from his Law and the forgiveness of God from the gospels, and then by the strength of the Holy Spirit saving faith will be embedded in your heart... Faith begins from the gospel. Without the gospel there cannot be faith, moreoever if you want, O Christian, to learn how to lead a holy life, to be a real Christian and not a false one, then open up the holy gospel, spread out the faultless life of Christ and learn from it.

St Tikhon's high view of the scripture is very typical of the Russian Orthodox today. The Bible is viewed with reverence, even with awe; people venerate the actual Gospel Book as they would an icon, for it is regarded as the icon of Christ. It is not uncommon to see, on the overcrowded underground trains, a young person reading a battered New Testament, and while few of the Orthodox I have met are able to quote chapter and verse or give the Bible the prominence which, for example, the Russian Baptists do, the children I taught from Orthodox families certainly knew Bible stories and were at home with the teaching of the Gospels.

The Russian Bible, Synodal Version, 1876

Which version did they read? That is another vexed question in Russia. In a preface to a new translation of Mark, John and Revelation which was prepared in 1997 by scholars in the Slavonic Bible Fund of the Russian Academy of Sciences and funded by the United Bible Societies, Metropolitan Philaret of Minsk wrote, 'Our Christian tradition has not been rich in translations of the Bible...'

Although in recent years there have been various modern translations of the Gospels and New Testament and one of the whole Bible, none has so far found favour with the established Christian churches, Baptist or Orthodox, nor in their seminaries. The established version of the Bible is the Synodal Text. The Slavonic Bible which had held sway in Russia until almost the end of the nineteenth century, and is still used in church services, was based on the Byzantine texts. However, in 1813, under the auspices of the newly established Bible Society of Russia, work was begun on a new translation. This society met with resistance from the highly conservative Russian authorities and was forcibly closed on the death of Tsar Alexander III in 1825. Not surprisingly, therefore, it took almost fifty more years before the Synodal Text appeared in 1876 and had its basis in the *Textus Receptus*, the Received Text of Erasmus of Rotterdam, who was the first to translate Greek texts from Byzantium, though he only had available later manuscripts than those from which the Slavonic Bible had been translated. The Russian of the Synodal Translation is often archaic, which makes it hard for contemporary young people to read, although Baptist friends of ours, reared on it from earliest childhood, love its very archaicness and defend it hotly against any attempts at modernization. In vain does one point out that biblical scholarship has moved on since the mid-nineteenth century, that there are more up-to-date ways of expressing words which have gone out of use in modern Russian; the Synodal Bible is the preferred version. Educated Orthodox readers like the *Brussels Bible* (1965, 1989 published by Life with God), which includes the Apocrypha and has a splendid commentary on the various books of the Bible, on biblical history and background and is a valuable aid to Bible study on one's own or in small groups. Father Alexander Men was one of the contributors to this work.

Children's thoughts on the Bible

I asked some children to express their thoughts on the Bible. An eleven-year-old girl wrote, somewhat precociously: 'I think the Bible something holy, unapproachable and hard to grasp right to the end. When I read it I forget about everything except the scriptures themselves and the Lord Jesus Christ.'

A twelve-year-old boy got on his soapbox and added: 'I think that the Bible is not merely a book. People should live their lives in accordance with its teachings in harmony, peace and love, just as the disciples of Christ did. I should like everyone to live like them and so I decided to write a poem which I have called 'The Bible':

> *You strengthen us when we are sad,*
> *when we've been offended by what someone has done.*
> *Sometimes I feel bitter and hate the whole world*
> *but then I open your holy pages*
> *and everything inside me catches fire and burns*
> *and I passionately want to love the whole world.*

This boy sang in a church choir. His father, a physicist, had not been promoted at work and had never been allowed to take part in international scientific conferences because it was known that he was a practising Christian. Maybe the youngster's wish that everyone should live like the first disciples sounds somewhat naive, but the same thought has been voiced by Metropolitan Anthony Bloom: 'It seems to me that the whole Christian world, including the Orthodox world, has departed from the simplicity, the wholeness and the joyful beauty of the gospel.'

A contemporary of Metropolitan Anthony, Father Alexander Ilyin (1895–1971), who spent many years in labour camps, taught his parishioners in Novogorod: 'It's necessary to read the Word of God regularly, little by little. It works in our organism like food, creating living cells in our souls... There is no greater strength for cleansing us of past sins than the reading of the Word of God.'

We have to recall that Father Ilyin was encouraging Bible reading in a country where the scriptures were virtually unobtainable. All but wiped out after the Revolution, precious pages were copied out by hand in total secrecy. A friend of ours in St Petersburg became a Christian after a scrap of paper with an extract from one of the Gospels somehow found its way into her hand. The secret nuns who nurtured Father Alexander Men, struggling for their very survival, hiding away with false papers, maintained their monastic life under insurmountable difficulties. Only some very elderly sisters were able to devote the time the Order laid down for Bible reading, but in spite of all their hardships the nuns read through the four Gospels without fail every Lent.

But for the mass of ordinary people, the Bible had disappeared from view and only crude distortions, taken out of context, were mockingly displayed in museums of atheism. The miracle is that people who were taught to believe that the Bible is an obscure batch of ancient and totally irrelevant texts have been able to approach the scriptures at all. In many cases, when my husband or I would tentatively suggest the reading of a psalm or a verse from one of the Gospels, while many friends soaked up the scriptures and started to read on their own, others would agree out of politeness—but we would feel as though we had brought in a bad smell!

For forty years no new Bibles were printed at all in Russia. Then in 1956 the Moscow Patriarchate received permission to publish the scriptures. It goes without saying that these were never put on general sale. Bibles came into Moscow and Leningrad only because believers, Baptist and Orthodox, were ready to lose their jobs, their living space, their freedom and make contact with Christians from the West who brought in as many Bibles as they could. Indeed, the copies which found their way on to the black market where they sold at exorbitant prices were those which customs officials had confiscated at entry points into the closed and silent world of the former USSR.

And, of course, outside the major cities there were almost no copies of the scriptures at all.

This makes the work of a Bible teacher like Father Alexander Men all the more remarkable.

We should read the holy scriptures every day, and that's especially true of the New Testament, which we can read in part or by chapters, just as we wish, or else choose passages which correspond to the lectionary of the Church for that particular day. It's good to read the Epistles along with an extract from the Gospels, and from the Old Testament we should read the psalms each day. It's better to read the other books of the Old Testament with the help of a commentary so that we may more correctly and more profoundly understand the meaning of the Old Testament books and their correspondence with the New...

But since it is 'out of the lips of children...' that God is praised (Psalm 8:2), I want to give the last voice in this chapter to the children I taught in St Petersburg in 1993 and 1994.

I think that the Bible is the best book in the world! It helps us to understand how to live in ways which please God. It's a book for grown-ups and children and it's very interesting to read. I think we all ought to study the Bible from childhood, just as they used to do in our country. In the Bible we can find a reply to any question, everything is foretold and explained. The Bible helps us find the meaning of life. Without doubt, this Book should be read by every single person—and then there will be peace on earth.

Polina, aged 13

The Bible is the book of God, the book which is distinct from all others. It is for every age and every generation. It is the voice of God—we hear his commands and covenants. If you're going through a difficult time in your life, you should turn to the Bible and you will find a reply to your problem. The Bible tells about the creation of the world, of humankind and of the coming of our Saviour, Jesus Christ, the Son of God. God loves us and wants us to live correctly—that's why he gives us his advice through the Bible.

Masha, aged 13

CHAPTER 11

Times and Seasons
THE ORTHODOX YEAR

ECCLESIASTES 3:1

For everything there is a season, and a time for every matter under heaven.

Although the apostle Paul, in his letter to the Galatians, has a few stern things to say to those who 'observe special days, and months, and seasons, and years' (4:10; see also Colossians 2:16), this was addressed to a specific concern in the days of the early Church: new Christians were still observing Jewish and pagan festivals and the requirement was plainly that a clean break should be made.

Observing the feast and the fast must have come back into the Church's tradition quite early on, for we have the celebration of Easter, linked, as it is, so closely to the Jewish Passover, the celebration of Christmas, put in December to coincide with—and 'convert'—the old pagan festivals of the Birth of Light.

It seems that human beings have a need to celebrate and commemorate. C.S. Lewis, reflecting on the Puritan culture in which Milton created his epic, *Paradise Lost*, wrote that when the Puritans threw out the maypoles and the mince pies, they didn't usher in the Millennium—on the contrary, they brought about the Restoration!

And when your children ask you, 'What do you mean by this observance?' you shall say, 'It is the passover sacrifice to the Lord, for he passed over the houses of the Israelites in Egypt...'
(Exodus 12:26–27)

The Old Testament definitely encourages the people of the first covenant to both celebrate and commemorate. Exodus 12:17–28

177

gives very precise instructions as to how the first and all subsequent Passovers were to be kept. The main festivals of the Old Testament calendar were: Passover, Pentecost, the Feast of the Atonement, the Feast of Tabernacles and the Feast of Shelters (Booths) as well as the two later festivals of Hanukkah and Purim. We read that the Lord blessed his people in their keeping of the feasts. 2 Chronicles 30 describes how the keeping of Passover was used to turn the whole nation back to the Lord: 'For the Lord your God is gracious and merciful, and will not turn away his face from you, if you return to him (v. 9). And indeed the Lord 'healed the people' (v. 20) and there was a time of great gladness and renewal. 'There was great joy in Jerusalem, for since the time of Solomon son of King David of Israel there had been nothing like this in Jerusalem. Then the priests and Levites stood up and blessed the people, and their voice was heard; their prayer came to his holy dwelling in heaven' (vv. 26–27).

We know that Jesus and his parents kept these festivals (Luke 2:41–42) and that the boy Jesus gave the Passover feast a special meaning (vv. 46–49). In John's Gospel we read of six occasions in which Jesus was in Jerusalem for various festivals (John 2:13–25; 4:43–45; 5:1; 7:1–51; 10:22–23; 12ff). Each of these festivals was an occasion for the Lord to give a special sign, special teaching—until in the end he gave himself.

A time to plant and a time to pluck up
what has been planted... (Ecclesiastes 3:2)

In Old Russia, the year began in September and revolved entirely around church fasts and festivals, giving rise to folk wisdom, mostly connected with the weather. In English we have, 'March comes in like a lion and goes out like a lamb'; old people used to warn, 'Ne'er cast a clout till May be out' and, 'Be buttoned up to chin till May be in...' Similarly in Russia: at New Year they said, 'The days lengthen as long as a hare leaps'; in February they prophesied, 'The deeper the snow, the better the harvest' and in July, 'When summer's wet, in autumn we'll fret'; 'If you don't sweat in summer, you'll not be warm in winter...' As in western Slav countries to this day, the months of the year were not the

Latin names used today—January, February and so on—but had much more descriptive names. January was 'the time when forests are cut'; February was 'cruel'; March was the 'birchy' month, and so on.

Until 1492, New Year began in spring. Then it was moved to 1 September and in 1700 Peter the Great brought New Year forward. However, the church calendar still begins on 1 September. Calendar changes have taken place in the West too: Pope Gregory XIII changed over to the Gregorian calendar in 1582, but in Russia the 'new style' was only introduced in 1918, so right up to the beginning of the twentieth century New Year's Day fell on 14 January. There's a difference of almost a fortnight between the two calendars. This explains why Christmas comes twelve days late in Russia and now follows New Year. Fir trees are not decorated until 31 December; presents are given then, and people party the night away. The New Year holiday overshadows Christmas, which comes as rather an anticlimax after the earlier celebrations. It is celebrated in church rather than in the home, in the same way that Harvest Festival is in Britain: after eighty years of non-observance of any Christian festival, people have lost touch with the old customs —which, in any case, tended to be secular, with overtones of Russia's pagan past. People went around the doors wassailing or mumming; young ladies with their maids anxiously tried to forecast the future, casting rings, putting candlewax into water: if it formed a letter, that could be the initial of a future sweetheart. Teenage girls would approach a mirror with trepidation—they might see not their own reflection but the face of their future husband.

We have seen his star… and have come to pay him homage. (Matthew 2:2)

The Church holds a six-week fast from the first Sunday in December, and Christmas Eve is traditionally a day of total fasting: no food was to be eaten until the first star twinkled in the frosty sky, in memory of the Star of Bethlehem. Twilight brought the household together to say their evening prayers. The older people would recount the Gospel story, and children and grown-ups together would praise the newborn king with singing, in some cases going from house to house with candles and with representations of the Christmas star. Then the church bells would ring. The sky came alive with the sound of bells and people took their lanterns and went to church, or prepared the festive table, first scattering straw over the table, then laying on top a crisply starched white cloth. No meat was allowed, but a special dish was made of the juice of almonds, buckwheat porridge or barley, poppyseed and honey.

I know this only from hearsay, but I can enter into it because in the old days before commercialism reached Poland I spent a never-to-be-forgotten Christmas there. The tree was dressed not with tinsel or fairy lights, but with dozens of little handmade straw stars. A scattering of straw covered the table beneath the crisp cloth and we waited with hungry anticipation for the shining of the star. I recall the hush and solemnity. There were no big, expensive presents. We greeted one another with a threefold kiss, breaking (and this is a Polish, not a Russian custom) a special Christmas wafer, which we offered to one another along with our best wishes for whatever life events, big or small, lay ahead in the coming year. Then we ate our meal with all those special non-meat dishes—there should be twelve in all—and went out across the snow to midnight Mass. People who are truly devout eat their first meal in the wee small hours, as the Orthodox do at Easter time.

Similarly, Christmas Eve in Old Russia used to be a family time but, in the days following, tables were laden and hospitality was offered to the extended family, to friends, to people on their own. Outside, it was midwinter, but within there was the good smell of roast meat: the family pig would have been slaughtered, providing sausages for the side dishes, as well as the main dish; the goose had been fattened and killed. Stoves burned brightly; the home was warm with the soft light of many candles; the *samovar* smoked and tea was served with honey, fragrant and sweet, and with root ginger, giving a rich, spicy smell.

The festivities lasted from 7 to 18 January. It was a time for old quarrels to be forgotten and forgiven, for peace and harmony to be sought among neighbours and friends. Peasant farmers took newborn lambs and calves into their homes; piglets and toddlers squirmed and squealed on the warm floor and babies were rocked in cradles, while the rich held balls and receptions. People dripped gold; diamonds gleamed and glinted on buttons and sword hilts of the men, on the ribboned awards and orders on their military breasts, in the ears, the hair, the skirts of the ladies, as well as on their fingers and wrists. But less exalted women loved jewellery too: a merchant's wife might have a belt made of pearls, a head-dress of gems as well as amber and coral beads.

'A time to dance...'

And, of course, the place to be at was the Tsar's wonderful Winter Palace on the banks of the Neva. The ballroom there was lit by ten thousand candles. Beneath the gleam of crystal chandeliers, across shining parquet floors, ladies and gentlemen danced their formal polonaises, their waltzes and quadrilles. Ladies in rustling silks, young bloods in sealskin trousers so tight that they had to be cut out of them, then wound their way along sumptuous corridors to the supper room aglow with the light of four thousand candles. The tables were set with priceless china. The whole room was filled with flowers. The heavy scent of camelias, gardenias and winter roses mingled with the fresh summer scent of oranges—for the salon had been turned into a bower: orange trees were twined in and among the tables and the guests sat under their shade.

The scene was perfect enchantment and eight hundred and fifty sat down to supper without the slightest confusion or squeeze. The Empress, according to the strict old etiquette of Russian hospitality, went round all the tables and spoke to each person until she fainted away... The colossal scale of everything... strikes the mind with wonder, while the kindness, cordiality and friendly hospitality of the people warm the heart. They are the most intelligent, agreeable, distingués, clever persons imaginable.

The *Russian Journal* (1836–37) of Lady Londonderry still strikes chords with people who enjoy Russian hospitality even in the lean post-Soviet era.

The Feast of Christ's Baptism

On 14 January, the Church observes the Circumcision of Christ; 18 January is a strict fast day, preceding the Feast of Christ's Baptism:

In those days Jesus came from Nazareth of Galilee and was baptized by John in the Jordan. And just as he was coming up out of the water, he saw the heavens torn apart and the Spirit descending like a dove on him. And a voice came from heaven, 'You are my Son, the Beloved; with you I am well pleased.'

(Mark 1:9–11)

On the Feast of the Baptism, frosts are expected. It was the talk of St Petersburg the year that there were none! It was 0°C. Everywhere was a mess of slush, treacherous underfoot, soaking even the most waterproof footwear. The canal banks looked sad, covered with dirty snow; water flowed over a thin coating of ice as though a clumsy cleaner had spilled muddy water over a dirty floor. The people were sad too. 'No frosts at the Baptism! This is terrible,' they all said. In the old days the Tsars made palaces of ice. Huge bonfires blazed on the river and the priests and people went out in procession with icons and singing to bore holes in the ice and draw up the water, which they would bless and keep in their homes all year... Nowadays they simply turn on the taps in the back of church! Safer that way, though less romantic. Everyone brings bottles and jars to fill with water which the priests have blessed in memory of Christ's baptism.

Babies were baptized by being plunged into the freezing water. A traveller in the eighteenth century witnessed the ceremony. He recalls how the priest, his hands doubtless numbed with cold, dipped a baby in—and dropped it. Far from showing horror, he simply turned to the waiting people: 'Next!' And the next parents brought their infant forward. The shocked observer turned to look at the bereaved couple. Tears streamed down their faces, but they were radiant. Exalted, they turned their gaze to the heavens, believing that their child had gone straight to glory with the saints and angels.

'Next!' That word seems to sum up for me all that is cruel in this country of great extremes, all that is puzzling in the faith of a people who direct their thoughts Godward and ignore the human dimension, who live in appalling single rooms while their churches and palaces shine with gold. I have written in my diary: 'One of the first Russian words I learnt was *uzhasno!*—'terrible'. The reality is that what is *uzhasno* is also *normalno*—'normal'!

The colour of hope...

Irina Ratushinskaya, in her prison memoir *Grey is the Colour of Hope*, relates how she and her half-starved fellow prisoners recalled the old Slav customs, reminded themselves that it was the feast of Christ's Baptism, stripped off their poor prison clothing, ran out into the freezing night air and rubbed themselves over with snow. The women came to no harm; on the contrary, they felt a great sense of physical and spiritual well-being.

This is still a great Russian passion: people assure me they keep well because they pour two buckets of cold water over themselves every morning. The Russian steam baths, with the plunge into a cold pool, is the city equivalent of the wooden bath house in the villages, where the session in the hot steam room, fragrant with the smell of pine, would be followed by a roll in the snow. Once when I was at the Russian *banya* (the baths), a six-week-old baby was plunged briefly into the cold bath—I heard his yells, and then saw him a few minutes later curled against his mother, wrapped with her under one sheet, deeply, contentedly asleep, his skin pink and glowing with health.

In Old Russia too, the Feast of the Baptism was a time when godparents, who were a very important part of every family, would gather with their godchildren, whose birthdays and name-days they would honour with gifts and prayers.

'My eyes have seen your salvation'

After the Baptism the next major festival is in February: the Feast of the Meeting, which commemorates the events in Luke 2:22–38: the infant Jesus is taken into the temple by his parents 'to present him to the Lord (as it is written in the law of the Lord, "Every firstborn male shall be designated as holy to the Lord"), and they offered a sacrifice according to what is stated in the law of the Lord, "a pair of turtledoves or two young pigeons".' Accordingly, Russian cooks that day used to bake pasties shaped like doves, swallows, skylarks, the harbingers of spring, for the old folk saying was, 'at the Feast of the Meeting spring and winter kiss…' Christ, the six-week-old baby, the Dayspring from on high (Luke 1:78, KJV) lies in the arms of the old man who is ready to die; and the Church celebrates the wonder of this: 'Let the doors of heaven open today: for the Word of the Father without beginning has entered time; not laying aside his divinity, as a forty-day-old infant born of the Virgin, he is freely carried by his mother into the lawful church: And now the old man takes him into his arms, saying "Lord, let your servant depart in peace, for my eyes have seen your salvation." Having come into the world to save the human race, O Lord, glory be to you.'

Saints' days

Entwined between the festivals which commemorate the gospel story there are saints' days, some common to the Western calendars of 'red-letter' days, others not. Lent is hard upon us, with the carnival feasting of *Maslenitsa* (Butter Week) preceding the lean days of the Great Fast. There is the great Feast of the Annunciation, which often falls mid-way to Easter, and afterwards, with brief spring soon giving way to summer, the Church celebrates the Ascension of the Lord, the Feast of the Holy Trinity, the Feast of the Apostles Peter and Paul and, in September, the Feast of John the Forerunner (the Baptist). There are two other major feasts connected with the Virgin which have no basis in scripture, but belong to the tradition of the Church: the Feast of the Dormition (the Assumption) of the Virgin, the Feast of the Birth of the Virgin. Another important Christ-centred festival comes in September with the Feast of the Lifting up of the Pure and Life-giving Cross of the Lord, a very ancient feast which dates back to the fourth century.

A 'what' culture, a 'why' culture

Anyone who reads twentieth-century Russian poets, particularly Akhmatova, Brodsky or Pasternak, will see how the liturgical year is so woven into their poetry that it is part and parcel of the imagery and even the choice of words. I have already suggested that in our increasingly fragmented society of high mobility and wealth on the one hand and social despair and homelessness on the other, a way forward for Christians to root our faith in the everyday world might well be, firstly, to return to the creation of 'drop-in centres for God'; secondly, to explore worship which uses our bodies as well as our minds; and, thirdly, to reclaim the rhythm of fasting as well as feasting. This, we have seen, provided social as well as religious glue to Eastern Europe as whole and Russia in particular, even during eighty years of total conformity to the atheistic state with its empty parades and meaningless ideology. In a recent study by Protestant missions working in the Middle East and therefore meeting with Orthodox Christians, it is suggested that Orthodox culture, with its liturgy and symbolism, is a 'what?' culture. People in a 'what?' culture (historically illiterate) ask, 'What did our forebears do? What does the Church teach?' They are concerned to honour the old traditions, to re-create, rather than reform, while Western Protestant churches were born in an increasingly literate, technological, rational and secular world which was concerned to ask, 'Why?' 'Why does the Church teach that? Why does the Bible say this?' (Turning Over a New Leaf: Protestant Missions and the Orthodox Churches of the Middle East, Interserve and Middle East Media, 1992).

So radical theologians pare down the essential Christian credos, denying the virgin birth on textual as well as natural grounds (Isaiah 7:14 is translated 'young woman', not 'virgin' in three out of the four modern English translations I use), denying even the resurrection and seriously disputing how much of the Gospels are actually what Jesus said or are really what the Church has said that he said... Yet against this background, and perhaps because of it, there is real spiritual hunger, a desire for the 'prayer of the heart', for stillness; yes, and for ceremony, for symbol and gesture as well as for cerebral assent to God, for worship which doesn't try to explain itself away. In all this we find well-springs of living water within the Orthodox tradition.

Russia's requiem

In 1962, when drab Soviet conformity held the huge landmass of the Union of Soviet Socialist Republics in its drear and fearful grasp, a painting by an established artist, Pavel Korin, shocked his compatriots. Three years later it was exhibited in America, where, again, out of all the paintings in the artist's personal exhibition, it attracted the most attention. And no wonder, because it was a picture which caught in full regalia the silenced and all but annihilated Russian church on a large canvas, one of two studies which were so big that the artist called them 'bas-profundo'. Its original title had simply been *Requiem*, but, following the advice of the Soviet writer, Maxim Gorky, Korin changed the title to *Vanishing Russia* and the word he chose for Russia was not *Rossiya*, but *Rus*, the holy Orthodox Russia which the Soviets sought to eliminate.

The work took decades. Korin worked on his sketches from 1930 to 1937, the most terrible years of Stalin's rule, but although the last portrait was painted in 1937 he continued with sketches for the vast composition until 1959. The catalyst to the picture was the funeral of Patriarch Tikhon in 1925. Patriarch Tikhon had tried to withstand Soviet pressure and had spent almost a year in prison. Although it was clear after his arrest that he was no longer free in his decision-making, he remained firmly non-political and said, 'The Russian Orthodox Church is non-political, and henceforward does not want to be either a Red or a White Church; it should and will be the One Catholic Apostolic Church, and all attempts coming from any side to embroil the Church in the political struggle should be rejected and condemned' (quoted *The Orthodox Church*, Timothy Ware, Penguin, 1963). Tikhon, knowing he could not live much longer, tried to nominate successors who would follow his clear Christian path, but both his nominees were done away with and his successor, Patriarch Sergius, as we have seen, enslaved the Orthodox Church.

*I will build my church, and the gates of Hades
will not prevail against it.* (Matthew 16:18)

Patriarch Tikhon died suddenly in his Moscow residence and thousands thronged the roads into Moscow for his funeral. The great tidal wave of silent humanity pressed its way onwards to pay last respects to the dead patriarch. Thus, in one of the many anomalies of Russian history, not least under the Soviets, there gathered together artists and musicians, but also the peasantry— not yet starved into collectivization, and the hidden prayer warriors of Russian life: the hermit monks and nuns. Pavel Korin was gripped by what he saw. Among the gold of the robes of bishops and priests were the hermits in austere black, whose gaunt faces and gnarled hands could have come straight from Rembrandt's late canvases. There were nuns veiled in black, with penetrating eyes; others whose gaze looked inward, perhaps foreseeing the hardships they were all about to endure. It was a wonder that they agreed to sit for the artist—and at first they refused. 'This is not God's work, son,' they said. But Korin found an ally in a retired bishop, Metropolitan Trifon, a member of a pre-revolutionary princely family, a man who was greatly loved by the believers of the day. Trifon agreed to sit, and although there were only four sessions in all, Korin not only caught his likeness, but caught the rest of the Russian Church too. For when they heard that the bishop had sat for Korin, the elders, elusive figures though they were, gave their consent. So, on the huge painting which Korin envisaged would hang in the erstwhile Cathedral of the Dormition in the Kremlin are the representatives of the Russian Church whose way of life was scheduled for immediate extinction; and in an oddly prophetic touch Korin put three Patriarchs together. In the centre stands Patriarch Tikhon, whose eyes stare out of his lean face beneath his crown as though he sees before him the barbed wire of the Gulag, the prisoners who lose teeth, hair, hope, health, whose skeletal bodies are thrown away, for there are always new slaves... To the right of Tikhon stands the man who betrayed the Church, Patriarch Sergius, who would die in 1944, and Patriarch Alexey (died 1970). In a prominent position beside these leaders Korin painted a 25-year-old monk-priest, Pimen, who would also lead the Church—thereby creating a pictorial history of the Orthodox Church under Communism.

The spirituality of this painting, however, lies in the vivid, individual portaits of monks and nuns whose lives of prayer were to be condemned as useless parasitism which should be discarded for ever. But it is this way of life which has endured and has enabled the captive Church to endure, and so in a very real sense, this piece of socialist realism, designed as a requiem for a church on the eve of demise, is in fact a token of its continuing power. 'You are Peter, and on this rock I will build my church, and the gates of Hades will not prevail against it,' declared the Lord (Matthew 16:18).

---

*The sun of righteousness shall rise,
with healing in its wings.* (Malachi 4:2)

The last picture I want to bring before you is a romanticized print from a journal printed in 1905. It is called *Returning from the Vigil*. Shrouded in darkness is a wooden church with two small, lit windows. Families are emerging from the church. Each one carries a lit flame which they carefully shield with their hands. This is the Paschal light. From it all the other lights in the house will be lit, and cowherds and dairy maids will carry the flame out to the byre to light the lanterns there too. They will exchange the joyful greeting, 'Christ is risen, truly he is risen!' This is a world without machinery, without electricity or paved roads. The women wear the high headdresses, shawls and long skirts of Old Russia; the men wear furs. Children are part of the procession too. There is weariness here—the Lenten fast has worn them down, the cold strikes chill, but the sky behind the towers and domes of the church is lit with a spreading band of dawn—the dawn of Easter, the dawn of all the world, of hope and of life eternal:

Desiring to save the world, O Dayspring from on High, having taken on yourself the darkness of our fallen nature, you humbled yourself to death; and so your Name has been exalted above every name and now you hear from the countless multitude from all tribes, peoples and languages in heaven and on earth this song of praise: Alleluia!'

Akathist to the Resurrection of Christ

BIBLIOGRAPHY

I have consulted or quoted from the following books and journals:

Valeria Alfeyeva, *Pilgrimage to Dzhvary*, trs. Stuart and Jenny Robertson (Lion Publishing, 1992)

Ilya Basin, *Chtenie Svyashchennogo Pisaniya* [Reading the Holy Scriptures], (ODSP-SU, Moscow, 1996)

John Bate, 'Rublev's Icon' (from *Touch of Flame*, Lion Publishing, 1989)

Julia de Beausobre, *Flame in the Snow* (on St Seraphim of Sarov), 1945

Ks. Mieczyslaw Bednarz SJ (ed.), *Skarbnica Modlitw* [*Treasury of Prayer*], (WAM Kraków, 1997)

Anthony Bloom, *Living Prayer* (Darton, Longman & Todd, 1966)

Maria Boulding, *The Coming of God* (SPCK, 1982)

Jerzy Braun (compiled and edited), *Poland in Christian Civilization* (Veritas Publications Centre, 1985)

David Brown, *Tchaikovsky, The Crisis Years* (Gollancz, 1982)

F. Cross (ed.) *The Oxford Dictionary of the Christian Church* (Oxford University Press, 1958)

Jane Ellis, *The Russian Orthodox Church, a Contemporary History* (Croom and Helm, 1986)

R. French (trs.), *The Way of a Pilgrim* (SPCK, 1954)

W.H. Frere, *Links in the Chain of Russian Church History* (Faith Press, 1918)

Grierson (ed.), *Gates of Mystery: the Art of Holy Russia* (Interculture and State Russian Museum)

Revd Thomas Hopko, *Osnovy Pravoslawiya* [*Basics of Orthodoxy*], (Polifakt, Minsk, 1991)

Turning Over a New Leaf: Protestant Missions and the Orthodox Churches of the Middle East (Interserve and Middle East Media, 1992)

E. Kadloubovsky and E.M. Palmer, *The Art of Prayer* (Faber, 1966)

Brother Kenneth CGA (Ed.), *From the Fathers to the Churches* (Collins, 1983)

Religion in Communist Lands, various volumes (Keston College)

Father John of Kronstadt, *Moya Zhizn' vo Christe* [*My Life in Christ*], (Pravoslavnaya Duchovnaya Akademiye, Leningrad, 1991)

L.P. Lyachovskaya, *Kalendar' slavyanskoy zhizni i trapezy* [*Calendar of Slavonic Life and Board*], Izdatel'skiy Dom MCP, Moscow, 1996

Suzanne Massie, *Land of the Firebird* (Simon and Schuster, 1980)

Memoirs of Father Alexander Men, *I bylo utro* [*And it was day*], A. Men Foundation, Moscow Vita-tsentr, 1992)

Father Alexander Men, *Kak chitat' Bibliyu,* [*How to Read the Bible*], (La Vie avec Dieu, 1981)

Father Alexander Men, *Prakischeskoe Rukovostvo k Molitve* [*Practical Handbook on Prayer*], (A. Men Foundation, 1991)

Father Alexander Men, *Radosnaya Vest'* [*Joyful News*], (Moscow Vita-tsentr, 1991)

Father Alexander Men, *Syn chelovecheskii* [*Son of Man*] (La Vie avec Dieu, 1968)

Vadim Nartsissov, 'Rus' Uchodyashchaya' ['The Passing Away of Holy Russia'] in *Nasledie* [*Heritage*], 1989

Henri Nouwen, *The Return of the Prodigal Son* (Darton, Longman & Todd, 1994)

'Ot Zautrenii' ['Returning from Early Morning Service'] in *Niva* [*Sphere of Daily Life*] no. 15, 1905

Leonid Ouspensky and Vladimir Lossky, *The Meaning of Icons* (St Vladimir's Seminary Press, 1952)

Rainer Maria Rilke, *Stories of God* (Sidgwick & Jackson, 1912)

Elizabeth Roberts and Ann Shukman (eds), *Christianity for the Twenty-First Century, the Life and Work of Alexander Men* (SCM Press, 1996)

Synesmos, the Journal of Orthodox Youth (Spring, Summer 1998, Bialystock, Poland)

Tertullian, *On prayer* (quoted in *V Mire Molitvy*, [*In the World of Prayer*], Prot M. Pomanzkiy (Holy Trinity Monastery, Jordanville, 1957)

S.V. Timchenko, *Russian Icons Today* (Sovremennik, 1994)

Andrzej Turczynski, *Mistrz niewidzialney strony* [*Master of the Unseen Side*] (W Drodze, Poznan, 1996)

G. Vzdornov, *Vologda* (Aurora Art Publishers, Leningrad, 1978)

Benedicta Ward, *The Desert of the Heart* (Darton, Longman &Todd, 1988)

Kallistos Ware, 'The Hesychasts' and 'The Eastern Tradition' in *A Study in Spirituality*, ed. Jones, Wainwright, Yarnold (SPCK, 1986)

Kallistos Ware and Mother Mary (trs.), *Lenten Triodion* (Faber, 1978)

Timothy (Kallistos) Ware, *The Orthodox Church* (Penguin, 1963)